Sixth edition
Copyright © 2011 Alastair Sawday Publishing Co. Ltd
Published in 2011 by Alastair Sawday Publishing

Alastair Sawday Publishing Co. Ltd,
The Old Farmyard, Yanley Lane,
Long Ashton, Bristol BS41 9LR, UK
Tel: +44 (0)1275 395430   www.sawdays.co.uk

ISBN-13: 978-1-906136-41-3

Series Editor: Alastair Sawday
Editorial Director: Annie Shillito
Publishing Manager: Jackie King
Editorial assistance: Carmen Cox, Rebecca Whewell
Writing: Nicola Crosse
Additional writing: Jo Boissevain, Carmen Cox
Photo processing: Alec Studerus, Philip Jansseune, Jo Boissevain, Carmen Cox
Cover design: Walker Jansseune
Maps: Maidenhead Cartographic Services
Printing: Butler Tanner & Dennis, Frome, UK
Production: Pagebypage Co. Ltd

Photography

Front cover: Mark Bolton
Back cover: Rob Cousins
Page 1: Photolibrary.com/Jo Whitworth
Page 6: Garden Pix Ltd /Photolibrary.com
Page 8: Lucy Pope
Page 9: Tom Germain
Page 10/11: Rob Cousins
Page 12: Lesley Chalmers
Page 15: Lucy Pope, Glendurgan, The Old Vicarage
Page 94: www.istockphoto.com/fotoVoyager
Page 97: Lucy Pope
Page 186: Lucy Pope
Page 189: Rob Cousins, Cambo House, Rob Cousins
Page 212: Lesley Chalmers
Page 215: Glendurgan, 24 Fox Hill, Barn Close
Page 240: Rob Cousins

Special Places to Stay
in Britain for

Garden Lovers

Foreword by
Tom Hodgkinson

● Special places to stay (with page numbers)

Contents

Foreword by Tom Hodgkinson
Editor of *The Idler*

The garden is the result of a harmonious collaboration between man and nature, and it should really be considered as our highest art form. The good garden offers beauty to all the senses. As Renaissance philosopher Francis Bacon put it: 'God Almighty first planted a garden. And indeed it is the purest of man's pleasures. It is the greatest refreshment to the spirits of man.'

This is all true, but gardens require a lot of hard work from human beings. I feel sure that in addition to the creative input from God Almighty, Adam and Eve must have had a considerable support staff in order to maintain Eden. Unless I am very much mistaken, you do not get gardens in nature. If you leave a garden alone, a weedy nightmare will result, very quickly indeed.

This was a point insisted upon by the great Roman poet Virgil in his fabulous didactic gardening poem, *The Georgics*, composed between the years of 37 and 30 B.C. Virgil himself had retired from the bustle of Rome to live on a commune where he was taught philosophy by Siro the Epicurean. The key note of the poem is the phrase *labor omnia vicit*, or 'hard work conquered everything'. Virgil says that the gardener is like a boatman rowing upstream: let go of the oars just for one moment, and the boat will be hurled back down the river. And, says the poet, unless you harry the weeds in your vegetable garden with unrelenting mattock, then you will be eating acorns all winter.

Yes, gardens are the happy result of imagination and creativity wedded to hard toil. We lazy ones are lucky, then, to be able to visit and enjoy the gardens in this lovely book without having to put the hard toil in ourselves. We can enter these sweet-smelling bowers and stately vegetable beds, stroll around the trim borders, smell the roses, eat a wild strawberry, read the Metaphysical poets, fall over in a lovesick swoon, and so refresh our spirits and senses; all without ever having to pick up a spade.

The other point to make about gardens is that they are all different and all reflect the personalities and interests of their owners and makers. The gardener has complete freedom to do whatever he or she wants to do. Alastair Sawday's *Garden Lovers* does a great service by collecting in one place these groves of pleasure and liberty, so we lazy aesthetes can enjoy them either from afar or in reality.

Introduction by Alastair Sawday

I am no gardener. So I am easily bowled over by the gardens of other people. I see them as pictures of creativity and hard graft. The human energy on show is prodigious. I know because I watch others working hard in our allotment. I am one of the spade-leaners, summoned from my reveries and convivial chats by one more horticulturally driven than I.

Perhaps allotments, brilliant invention that they are, fail to generate the romanticism of gardens. They are largely for vegetables. Only in a proper garden do you have the free rein to invent, to bring your fantasies down to the earth. That is why it is such fun being able to wander at will around the gardens of others. Each one is like an art gallery, with the bonus of each creation enabled by the hidden hand of nature.

Last year I spent a while in one of our B&Bs on the shore of Lake Maggiore, in Italy. The owner is a devoted collector of pine trees. I was enchanted as much by his mad-cap enthusiasms as by his collection. I had thought little about pines, but as one species yielded to another I was hooked. There were giants and pygmies, pines pretending to be mangrove with their feet in the lapping waves of the lake, soft-grey pines appearing to float in the air and sharp ones that protected the garden. Pines had been brought from the Himalayas. Being there was an experience. A simple B&B weekend had become something more.

Britain, with its vast gardening tapestry, has a thousand of these experiences to offer – if not with pines. This book is a teaser and I love the sheer miscellany of it. You can puff up your gardening ambitions one weekend in a grand estate's garden, and bring yourself to earth the next in a tiny cottage garden. In them all you can swap tips with the owners, eat the freshest of vegetables, admire the rarest of plants, learn either from experts or inspired amateurs – and top up your enthusiasms. They are indeed, as Tom so delightfully observes in his foreword, 'groves of pleasure and liberty'.

Forty-three of these wonderful places allow you to stay all day – in even the kindest of historic gardens you are, quite reasonably, invited to leave at the end of the day; in these you can linger over drinks, dinner and bedtime. The day – with its pleasures and liberties – is yours.

We have dramatically changed the book's format to allow for more and better photographs. Inside, you will find hotels, self-catering houses and B&Bs, and delightful people eager to share their enthusiasms and their gardens. And of course you will also find very beautiful and comfortable places to stay.

Alastair Sawday

Practical information

How we choose our Special Places
Those who are familiar with our Special Places series know that we look for comfort, originality and authenticity, and reject the anonymous and the banal. The way guests are treated comes as high on our list as the setting, the architecture, the atmosphere, food and, of course, the garden. We visit every place to get a feel for how both house and owner tick. It's all very informal, but it gives us an excellent idea of who would enjoy staying there.

Subscriptions
Owners pay to appear in this guide. Their fee goes towards the high costs of inspecting, of producing an illustrated book and maintaining a website. We only include places that we like and find special - it is not possible for anyone to buy their way in.

Disclaimer
We make no claims to pure objectivity in choosing these places. They are here simply because we like them, and we hope you will like them too. We have done our utmost to get our facts right but apologise unreservedly for any mistakes that may have crept in.

You should know that we don't check such things as fire regulations, swimming pool security or any other laws with which owners of properties receiving paying guests should comply. This is the responsibility of the owners.

Feedback
In between inspections we rely on feedback from our army of readers. This feedback is invaluable to us and we always follow up on comments.

Maps
Each entry has a page number this is used on the key map on p4 and on the regional maps that you'll find here: p14 (South West & Wales), p96 (South East & Central), p188 (The North) and p214 (Scotland).

Ethical Collection
We're always keen to draw attention to owners who are striving to have a positive impact on the world. Over 20 entries in this book belong to our 'Ethical Collection'. Their owners are working hard to reduce their environmental footprint, or are making significant contributions to the community; others are passionate about serving local or organic food.

Sawday's Travel Club
Over half these places have joined the Travel Club. You'll see details of various Travel Club offers throughout the book that range from malt whisky in your room to a drive in a carriage with a pair of Dartmoor ponies!

Types of places
We include B&Bs, hotels and self-catering places. Under

each entry we tell you whether a room is a double, twin/double (ie. with zip and link beds), suite (with a sitting area), family or single. Many bedrooms have an en suite bath or shower, but please check on booking. Self-catering entries may include a studio for two or a cottage for four. Note, it is rare to be given your own room key in a B&B.

Meals

Unless we say otherwise, a full cooked breakfast is included. Often you will feast on local sausage and bacon, eggs from resident hens, home-made breads and jams. In some you may have organic yogurts or cheeses and ham.

Apart from breakfast, no meals should be expected unless you have arranged them in advance. The same goes for packed lunches. Meal prices are quoted per person, and note that meals in a B&B are often a social occasion shared with your hosts and/or other guests.

Prices and minimum stays

Each entry gives a price per room for two. We also include prices for singles where available. The price range covers a one-night stay in the cheapest room in low season to the priciest in high season. Some owners charge more during regattas, festivals etc, and some charge less for three-night stays. Some owners ask for a two-night minimum stay at weekends.

Booking and cancellation

Be clear about the room booked and the room and meal price. Requests for deposits vary; some are non-refundable, and some owners may charge you for the whole of the booked stay in advance. Some cancellation policies are more stringent than others; some owners will take the deposit directly from your card without contacting you to discuss it. So ask them to explain

their cancellation policy clearly before booking so you understand exactly where you stand.

Symbols

Please use them as a guide rather than an absolute statement of fact (things can change) and check anything that is important to you.

&#9855;	Bedroom/bathroom accessible for wheelchairs
	Bedroom/bathroom accessible without steps
	Children of all ages welcome
	Your pet can stay in your bedroom
	The owner has pets
	Owner can pick up from station/arrange collection
	Most credit cards accepted
	Good vegetarian dinner options
	WiFi access
	Bikes to hire or borrow
	Tennis court
	Swimming pool

Cornwall • Devon • Dorset • Somerset • Bristol • Bath & N. E. Somerset
Wiltshire • Gloucestershire • Powys • Gwynedd • Flintshire

England: South West & Wales

England: South West & Wales

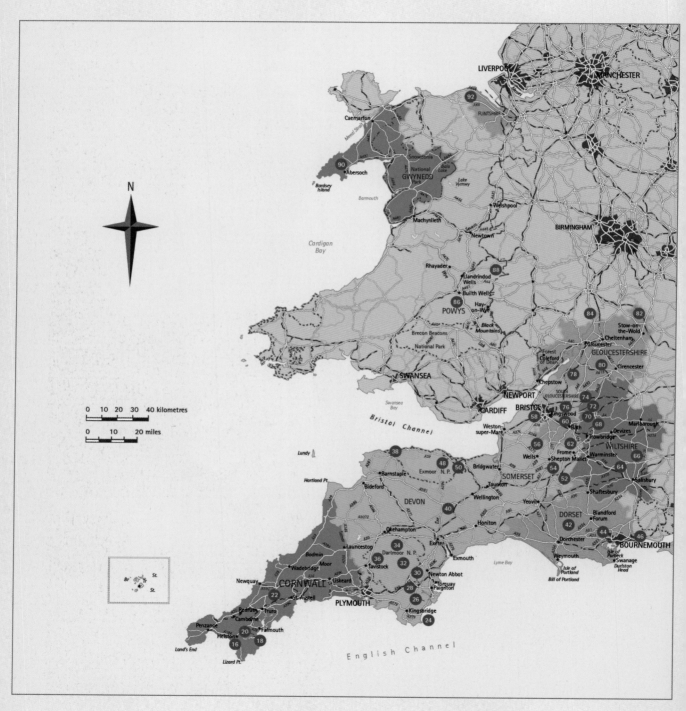

Special places to stay

Mazey Cottage

A wild valley garden interspersed with impeccable swathes of planting

The house

Descend into a wooded valley to a cluster of chocolate-box Cornish cottages. Marion and Peter, warm, kind and able, give you breakfast bacon from Retallack, scrambled egg with salmon, fresh fruit, and homemade jams. Your cosy bedroom – not huge but in its own 'wing' – is in French boudoir style, with crisp cotton and soft down; the new bathroom is roomy and you have your own sitting room with a wood-burning stove for chilly evenings. You are on the Penrose Estate for lovely walks; Peter is a keen canoeist and can offer a kayak on the Helford to the experienced. A great escape.

The garden

Marion "I garden for love" is modest, but she knows how to create something magical. Three-and-a-half acres of valley, a lot of which is native oak woodland by a small river, has been nurtured and cajoled into a magnificent smorgasbord of mowed grassland, wild grassland (with native flowers), sculptural installations, benches, seats, a summerhouse for lounging and a house terrace for outdoor breakfasts. Peter does the hard mowing, Marion is the plants person and she's divided the garden into different areas without destroying the natural feel: a small ancient oak wood runs along the stream and forms one side, with wooden bridges that lead back to open areas. There's a wild feel interspersed with impeccable beds, planted in swathes for colour and scent: a vegetable patch with raised beds is neat as a pin, and at the end of the walk is the raised summerhouse with a deck area for hot and dry Mediterranean succulents. A large natural pond is for dreaming by, there are rare wild plants in spring, and mature trees for seeking shade. Wildlife abounds; otters, badgers, foxes, mink, eels, bats and buzzards make it their home. Any sign of hard work is muted into the landscape that inspired the garden. Clever indeed. *NGS*.

Details

- Rooms: 1 twin/double.
- Price: From £90. Singles £50.
- Meals: Pub/restaurant 1 mile.
- Travel Club offer: Free pick-up from local bus/train station.
  Local food/produce in your room.

On your doorstep
- Trevarno: the estate is a picture in May with bluebells & rhododendrons; take tea in the subtropical Garden Conservatory
- Bonython Estate: three lakes reflect varied planting, as Cornish variety apples ripen in the orchard

Top tip
Work with, not against, your landscape, soil conditions & climate

Contact

Marion Stanley
Mazey Cottage,
Tangies, Gunwalloe,
Helston TR12 7PU

01326 565868
stanley.m2@sky.com
www.mazeycottage.co.uk

Map: see page 14

Glendurgan

Magical Victorian wooded valley with plants from all over the world

The house

In 1827 a thatched cottage stood where the light-filled family house now surveys the valley. Charles's paintings of plants and trees line the well-lit stairwell and there are family furniture, books and paintings galore. You eat well: Caroline trained as a cook and her breakfasts draw on the best of local and homemade. Bedrooms have sensational south-facing views; Violet, next to the bathroom, and Magenta, a few yards down the corridor, are as your Edwardian aunt would have liked. No TV but a grand piano, and the view to Helford river through the glen is stunning.

The garden

Three Fox brothers created valley gardens near Falmouth in the 1820s: Robert: Penjerrick; Charles: Trebah; Alfred: Glendurgan – which, in 1962, was donated to the National Trust. It's a magical, exotic, heavily shrubbed and wooded place, the tulip trees are some of the largest and oldest in Europe, and there's a sense of fun and discovery as you wend down on steep, superbly maintained paths (pebble-cobbled, bamboo-balustraded) to take a breather on Durgan beach – before climbing back up the other side. It is splendidly scented in spring with camellias, bluebells, primroses and lime-tree flowers. Summer, to quote Charles's excellent book, "breaks in a wave of whiteness, with eucryphia, hoheria, myrtus and that 'bombe Alaska' of rhododendrons, 'Polar Bear', while autumn is awash with bulbs such as amaryllis, colchicum, crinum and nerine." In the winter this is still an important garden in terms of its collection of fine trees, and, even in the wildest weather, a deeply romantic place to be. There is much to explore, including an ancient laurel maze, and Charles will tell you all you want to know; he is a garden designer, trained at Kew and the Inchbald School of Garden Design, and leads garden tours. *Garden owned by the National Trust.*

Details	Contact

• Rooms: 2 twins.
• Price: From £90. Singles £75.
• Meals: Restaurant 2 miles.

On your doorstep
• Trebah Gardens: daffodils & magnolia at Easter, heavenly Hydrangea Valley in summer
• Potager Garden: a lush summer tangle of flowers, vegetables, fruit trees, a vegetarian café & foraging courses

Top tip
For maximum impact, cram as many narcissi in a pot as you can

Charles & Caroline Fox
Glendurgan,
Mawnan Smith,
Falmouth TR11 5JZ

01326 250326
fox@glendurgan.plus.com

Map: see page 14

Cornwall

Carwinion

Fourteen acres of majestic bamboo in an unmanicured river valley garden

The house

Come for the setting. This rambling manor began life in 1790 and was enlarged in the 1840s. Inside: a faded grandeur and a characterful collection of oddities (corkscrews, penknives, magnifying glasses) that successive generations have handed down. Your hosts invite you to share their home with its big old bedrooms and bathrooms (not swish). The only sound you'll hear here is the bamboo growing – from that wonderful wild, earthy, primal garden. The walk down to the beach is magical. *Min. two nights bank holiday weekends. Smoking allowed in parts of the house.*

The garden

If an inquisitive, errant dinosaur were to come rustling out of the great stands of bamboo or soaring gunnera, you might not be that surprised. These 14 acres are a ravishing homage to leaf, foliage, wildness... a heavenly place of trees, ponds, streams. No wonder that Jane, who has done so much for these grounds in recent years, calls it an "unmanicured garden." At the end of the 19th century, Anthony's grandfather planted the first bamboos in this gorgeous valley garden leading down to the Helford River. Today Carwinion has one of the finest collections in Europe, more than 200 species with wonderful leaf and stem forms...

members of the Bamboo Society of Great Britain flock here for annual get-togethers. The lushness soars impressively to the sky – don't miss the 20-foot pieris. Jane has made a series of paths to lead you through one breathtakingly romantic area after another, a palm sheltering under a tall beech tree, a banana tree thriving in the mild atmosphere. Tree ferns soar and, in a final flourish at the foot of the garden, she has transformed an old quarry into an enchanting fern garden. Springtime's azaleas and rhododendrons are a joy. Magic everywhere. *NGS, RHS, Good Gardens Guide.*

Details

- Rooms: 1 double, 2 twins/doubles.
- Price: From £90. Singles £50.
- Meals: Occasional dinner.
  Pub 400 yards.
- Travel Club offer: Free drinks with dinner.

On your doorstep
- Trebah Gardens: huge exotic paradise all year round & child/dog friendly, too
- Glendurgan: superb exotic gardens, 176-year-old cherry laurel maze & the 'Giant's Swing'

Top tip
When buying bamboo, note whether it's a spreader or a clumper

Contact

Jane Rogers
Carwinion,
Mawnan Smith,
Falmouth TR11 5JA

01326 250258
jane@carwinion.co.uk
www.carwinion.co.uk

Map: see page 14

Tregoose

Romantic summer borders &
potager – and spectacular
woodlands with snowdrops

The house

Tregoose is a handsome, late-Regency country house
surrounded by rolling countryside. In the drawing
room, where a log fire is lit on cooler evenings, a rare
and beautiful Chinese cabinet occupies one wall
and in the dining room is a Malayan inscribed silk
screen – a thank you present from Empire days.
Lovely, comfortable, period bedrooms have antique
furniture, views onto the garden and pretty
bathrooms with generous baths. At the head of the
Roseland Peninsula yet conveniently near the A390
this is a great ensemble: house, garden, hosts and
charming pets. *Children by arrangement.*

The garden

Alison, who grew up in Cornwall, has an NDH and has created a lovely garden – formal at the front, wilder to the rear and side – that opens to the public thrice yearly. Five fat Irish yews and a tumbledown wall were the starting point... but having reconstructed the walls to create a sunken garden, things started to look up. The L-shaped barn was a good backdrop for planting, so in went cotinus and yellow privet, flame-coloured alstroemerias, show-stopping *Crocosmia solfaterre* (bronze leaves, apricot yellow flowers) and blue agapanthus for contrast. The sunken walled garden protects such tender treasures as A*loysia citrodora*, *leptospermum*, and, pièce de résistance, *Acacia baileyana purpurea*. Palm-like dracaena, Monterey pines and cypresses and the Chusan palm do well, and you can't miss the spectacular magenta blooms of the 30-foot *Rhododendron arboreum* 'Cornish Red'. The woodland garden displays more muted colours, scented deciduous azaleas, and the white July-scented rhododendron 'Polar Bear'. Over 60 varieties of snowdrop flower from November to March – spectacular. The potager supplies produce for dinners and flowers for the house, and Alison can supply almost any information about Cornish plants and gardens. *NGS, Cornwall Garden Society.*

Details

- Rooms: 2 doubles, 1 twin.
- Price: From £98.
- Meals: Dinner from £28. BYO. Pub/restaurant 1 mile.

On your doorstep
- Caerhays Castle: superb magnolias, camellias & rhododendrons within earshot of the surf
- Poppy Cottage: small but cleverly designed plantsman's garden, & wildfowl in the orchard

Top tip
Lift, divide & replant snowdrops just as the shoots emerge

Contact

Alison O'Connor
Tregoose,
Grampound,
Truro TR2 4DB

01726 882460
www.tregoose.co.uk

Map: see page 14

Higher Beeson House

Big plants, woodland walks, water, views and tranquil seating spots

The house

The 16th-century farmhouse and stables, arranged around a neat yard, have been kitted out with ground-source underfloor heating and natural slate floors. Lynda and Charles give you a great local breakfast in the beamed dining room with views through the kitchen to the garden. Bedrooms are in the stables: enter through a green tiled hall where there is a drying room and a communal fridge for fresh milk or a bottle of wine. All are a good size, newly carpeted, spotlessly clean and with good lighting. Find the chic summerhouse by the lake, replete with wood-burning stove and comfy chairs.

The garden

There's lots going on here. What started as four acres of boggy wilderness which Lynda and Charles hoped would 'gradually evolve' has become a super garden that is clearly loved. It started with the pond, now stocked with rudd, visited by mallards and moorhens, and packed with flag irises and lilies. Then a series of steps and terraces (all built by clever Charles), bubbling fountains, timber decks, a waterfall, and a greenhouse. Lynda is the plantsman and she goes for big plants! Gunnera, bamboo, echiums and a banana plant all zoom heavenward while yuccas, phormiums and agapanthus add to the exotic feel. In the perennial bed there are more traditional plants like roses and stocks. The gentle climate allows bougainvillea and hibiscus to grow alongside a vine and a fig, and even olives in a sheltered spot. Vegetables, soft fruit and herbs grow happily, and the greenhouse produces chillies and sweet peppers in abundance. There are willows and alders around the pond and spruce, firs, oaks, ash, chestnut and rowan in the woodland area. So peaceful, so much wildlife; pick a bench and delight in it all. Sometimes you can hear the sea.

Details

- Rooms: 3 doubles.
- Price: £80-£94.
- Meals: Dinner, 3 courses, £25. Pub/restaurant 0.75 miles.

On your doorstep
- Overbecks: a lush tropical paradise in an unusually balmy climate, with breathtaking coastal views
- South West Coast Path: join up with 630 miles of wonderful walkways for matchless scenery & wildlife

Top tip
Encourage ducks for slug control

Contact

Lynda & Charles Rogers
Higher Beeson House,
Beeson, Kingsbridge TQ7 2HW

01548 580623
07977 905836 (mobile)
enquiry@higherbeeson.co.uk
www.higherbeeson.co.uk

Map: see page 14

Greenswood Farm

Two acres of beds, ponds &
pathways in a hidden valley

The house

A lovely Devon longhouse covered in wisteria, with stone flagging, deep window sills, elegant furniture. But this is a working farm and there is no stuffiness in Helen and Roger; this is a warm and cosy place to relax and enjoy the valley that is now their patch. You have a separate staircase to sunny bedrooms with garden views, huge mirrors, colourwashed walls, old pine and pretty fabrics. Organic beef and lamb are reared on the farm and breakfast eggs come from Sally Henny Penny outside. Buy some to take home – if you can drag yourself away. *Min. two nights in summer.*

The garden

Roger has a huge interest in countryside management, having worked on The Coast Path and restoring Green Lanes in the South Hams. Helen adores growing flamboyant flowers (and arranges them skilfully in the house). When they moved here eleven years ago they inherited a large garden planted on a boggy field with a stream running through and some mature shrubs and trees. Enlarged and landscaped, it has been designed to reflect the contours of its hilly, wooded outer borders. Perfect beds and borders are packed with spring bulbs, primroses, rhododendrons and azaleas, and pathways and older beds have been discovered and restored.

Water lovers such as the gigantic *Gunnera manicata*, white irises, ferns and grasses hug the ponds while there are delightful secret pathways through colourful borders with large shrubs; new paths take you across the fields and through the woods to another pond, or through a bluebell wood, over the fields and back to the house. Terracing some of the steeper areas has created quiet places to sit and take in the views. The orchard is being restored, the planting around the ponds developed; the final pond is on level ground, hidden from the house with views of Greenswood Valley. Birdsong, ancient woodland, glorious peace.

Details

- Rooms: 2 doubles, 1 twin.
- Price: From £80. Singles from £65.
- Meals: Pubs/restaurants 1.5 miles.
- Travel Club offer: Afternoon cream tea and cakes, bottle of wine in your room, for stays of 2+ nights.

On your doorstep
- Local country lanes: an English spring would be a dull thing without primroses
- Coleton Fishacre: rare & delicate plants thrive in the extraordinarily mild climate of this coastal garden

Top tip
Choose shrubs that flourish in your conditions & cover large areas

Contact

Helen Baron
Greenswood Farm,
Greenswood Lane,
Dartmouth TQ6 0LY

01803 712100
stay@greenswood.co.uk
www.greenswood.co.uk

Map: see page 14

7 The Grove

A patchwork cottage garden
in the heart of Totnes

The house

In the heart of lovely, higgledy-piggledy Totnes is a whitewashed house with pert blue windows and doors, friendly Bethan and John, homemade biscuits, pretty flowers and good art. Guests have an open-plan room, painted white, for delicious breakfasts of homemade bread and jam, local bacon and eggs, soft fruit from the garden. Bedrooms are light, bright and uncluttered (one with its own little sitting room), with wooden floors, excellent beds and handsome rugs; the bathroom bulges with big fluffy towels. And you can walk to Dartington along the river.

The garden

John and Bethan set out to create a peaceful and sheltered space in the middle of a busy and lively town – but they have done more than that. Here is an enchanting garden of surprises which all are welcome to roam. It's about a quarter of an acre in size and begins with a small courtyard area filled with pots, then up more steps to three small ponds, fed by rainwater from the house, and supplying the garden with frogs and newts. Beyond these are riotous flower beds separated by grass in which wildflowers are allowed to romp – dandelions, primroses, daisies. John is tolerant with the slugs and encourages the self-seeded to survive. Poppies, rocket, honesty,

hollyhocks, forget-me-nots and columbine rub shoulders with more formal planting; fruit and fir trees provide shade and roses, honeysuckle, clematis and blackberries scramble up walls. In summer the greenhouse groans with tomatoes and grapes, along with hibiscus, oleander and a bright red geranium. Behind a large stone wall there is a vegetable and fruit garden where priority is given to produce that is good to pick at and eat raw. Bethan and John love the garden but don't try to control it too much; they are more interested in creating shapes and spaces, appreciating light, shade and the seasons, and watching wildlife. Bliss.

Details		Contact
• Rooms: 2 twins/doubles. • Price: £80. Singles £50. • Meals: Pubs/restaurants 300 yards.	**On your doorstep** • Staverton: lovely snowdrops along the banks of the Dart • Greenway: visit Agatha Christie's house & gardens (by boat!); the wild, tumbling grounds hold camellias, magnolias & a restored vinery	Bethan Edwards & John Paige 7 The Grove, Totnes TQ9 5ED 01803 862866 totnesgrove@yahoo.com www.totnesgrove.com
	Top tip Plant 'Aquadulce' broad beans in Nov for an early crop without black fly	Map: see page 14

Devon

Kingston House

Fine historic gardens in perfect keeping with an 18th-century house

The house

Gracious and grand is this impeccably restored former home of a wealthy wool merchant with all its trappings intact: a rare marquetry staircase, an 18th-century painted china closet, marble works, original baths, galleried landings and oak panelling. But it's not austere – the bedrooms are steeped in comfort and cushions, a fire roars in the guest sitting room (formerly the chapel), food is fresh, delicious, home-grown; breakfasts are outstanding. Rugged Dartmoor is to the north, Totnes minutes away and walks from the house through the gentle South Hams are spectacular.

The garden

The whole place is an absolute gem for purists and nature lovers alike. Elizabeth's love of wildlife has made restoring the garden no easy task – she is adamant that no pesticides be used – but most of the estate was in need of a complete overhaul when she arrived. Now it is perfectly renovated and opens for the National Gardens Scheme four times a year: a rosy walled garden with peaches, pears, greengages and nectarines intertwined with roses and jasmine, beech hedging with yew arches, a formal rose garden, box topiary, a dear little summer house edged with lavender, an orchard with rare apples, and, in the South Garden, an avenue of pleached limes underplanted with tulips (illustrated here) leading to a wild woodland. Elizabeth is also a stickler for historical accuracy. New projects include a fountain and mulberry garden and a huge patterned box parterre for either side of the front drive (4,000 plants were propagated on site) interplanted with conical yews and parrot tulips for the spring – the height of fashion when the house was built! The vegetable garden is productive and neat with a nod to the contemporary – unusually shaped twigs and branches are used as natural sculptures for supporting beans and sweet peas. *NGS.*

Details

- Rooms: 2 doubles, 1 twin/double.
- Price: £180-£200.
  Singles from £110.
- Meals: Dinner, 3 courses, £38.
- Travel Club offer: 2 nights for the price of 1 or 3 nights for the price of 2. Dinner must be booked and paid for on one evening at £38 per person.

On your doorstep
- Dartington Hall Gardens: 20th-century gardens very fine in spring; the hybrid Lucombe Oak near the churchyard stays evergreen in milder years; the Great Lawn's crocus circle signals the end of wintry chill

Top tip
To get rid of aphids, spray roses with soapy water

Contact

Michael & Elizabeth Corfield
Kingston House,
Staverton,
Totnes TQ9 6AR

01803 762235
info@kingston-estate.co.uk
www.kingston-estate.co.uk

Map: see page 14

Corndonford Farm

Little farm garden with a wild profusion of cottage garden plants

The house

Come to be engrossed in the routines of a wild, engagingly chaotic haven. Ann and Will are friendly, kind and extrovert; guests adore them – and Beth the black labrador – and keep coming back. There is comfort, too: warm curtains, a four-poster with lacy drapes, early morning tea. Gentle-giant shire horses live at the shippon end where the cows once stood, and there's medieval magic with Bronze Age foundations. A wonderful place for those who love the rhythm and hubbub of real country life – and the Two Moors Way footpath is on the doorstep. *Children over ten by arrangement.*

The garden

Climb and climb the Dartmoor edge with views growing wider and wilder all the time until you reach the stone-walled lane and the sturdy granite buildings of Corndonford Farm. Roses and wisteria clamber up the rugged façade, softening the ancient strength of the house. At jam-making time the air is filled with the sweetness of an enormous pan of bubbling strawberries. Ann's jewel-like little farm garden has an arched walk of richly scented honeysuckle, roses and other climbers which leads to her very productive vegetable and soft fruit garden – the source of the berries. She knows her plants and has created a small, cottagey garden in complete harmony with its surroundings. There's a rockery and a little gravelled patio just outside the house which has been planted with charming cottage flowers. Above is a lawn edged by deep borders absolutely packed with colour and traditional cottage garden plants, including salmon-pink rhododendron, cranesbill and delphiniums. Do take the short walk along the lane to Ann's second garden, known locally as the "traffic calmer". Here, by the roadside, she has planted loads of rhododendrons and shrubs in a delightful display – and it really does encourage even the most hurried motorists to slow down. The views are breathtaking, the setting wonderfully peaceful, the garden as informal and welcoming as Ann and Will themselves.

Photographs © Tracey Elliot-Reep, Sophia Walcot

Details

- Rooms: 1 double, 1 twin.
- Price: £70. Singles £35.
- Meals: Pub 2 miles.
- Travel Club offer: Late checkout (12pm). Drive in carriage with pair of Dartmoor Hill ponies.
- Ethical Collection: Food. See page 10.

On your doorstep
- The Garden House: unforgettable garden surrounding the romantic ruins of a vicarage
- Stone Lane Gardens: 'The Mythic Garden': arboretum open all year

Top tip
When planting broad beans & peas, line trench with trimmed horse mane to deter moles & mice

Contact

Ann & Will Williams
Corndonford Farm,
Poundsgate,
Newton Abbot TQ13 7PP

01364 631595
corndonford@btinternet.com

Map: see page 14

Devon

Gidleigh Park

Acres and acres of rugged spaces, secret gardens, pathways & vegetable terraces

The house

Gidleigh Park is a perfect place, ten out of ten on all counts. Inside this faultless country house a fire smoulders in the oak-panelled hall and sofas come crisply dressed in dazzling fabrics. Bedrooms are divine, impeccably presented with hand-stitched linen, woollen blankets, upholstered headboards and polished wooden furniture. Back downstairs, beautiful art adorns the walls, while summer life spills onto a view-filled terrace. As for the food, Michael Caines brings two Michelin stars to the table, so expect the best – and sublime service from the loveliest staff. Matchless.

The garden

Bang in the middle of Dartmoor National Park, Gidleigh Park stands in 107 lush acres of garden and woodland; the North Teign river, with salmon and brown trout, meanders through and sweeping views shoot off to heather-wrapped Meldon Hill. Pull on your boots for dreamy walks: down the avenue of pollarded limes, over the Monet-style bridge, through the wildflower meadow and into the woodlands. Most trees here are over a hundred years old – magnificent copper beeches, ash, oak, Douglas firs – although sadly some were lost to a wintry cold snap. In spring, seven glorious acres of bluebells soothe the soul, but there's much to see all year round and guided walks point you in all directions: spot kingfishers, treecreepers, nuthatches, buzzards and deer. From the terrace peonies, lupins, tulips and alliums tumble down 'rockery style' to a sweet grotto and wishing well – probably built in the 1920s. Borders are packed with colour from azaleas, camellias, rhododendrons: chat about it all with head gardener Andy, veteran of 15 years and the architect of the granite-walled vegetable garden; much of the crop is picked for the kitchen. There's more: tennis court, croquet lawn, bowling green, 18-hole putting course and, best of all, quiet corners to sit in the sun.

Details

- Rooms: 21 twins/doubles, 3 suites.
- Price: £310-£500.
  Suites £550-£1,175.
- Meals: Lunch £37-£47.50.
  Dinner £99.
  8-course tasting menu £120.

On your doorstep
- The rugged Dartmoor landscape: spectacular in every season
- Stone Lane Gardens: on the edge of Dartmoor, the National Collection of Birch & Alder trees

Top tip
A water feature will attract frogs & toads, who in turn will gobble your slugs

Contact

Sue Williams
Gidleigh Park,
Chagford,
Newton Abbot TQ13 8HH

01647 432367
gidleighpark@gidleigh.co.uk
www.gidleigh.com

Map: see page 14

The Annexe, St Raphael

A sweet surprise round every corner – and creative inspiration

The house

Your diminutive south-facing annexe is an addition to Pat and Dave's restored miller's cottage. Sheep wool insulation and Dartmoor slate keep the feel local; a bedhead recycled from a local shop counter and colourful abstracts by an artist friend add originality, and pretty jugs of wild flowers give a homely touch. Step straight into the Shaker-style bedroom which doubles as your sitting area. There's a small kitchen too where you can do imaginative things with ingredients found at Tavistock's bi-weekly farmers' market. Cycle route 27 passes close by and walkers will be in moor-heaven.

The garden

As you pass by the ancient cider press and make your way through the enchanting garden the anticipation grows. A quirky mix of neat planting, granite pillars, salvaged finds and hand-made folly, it's a delight to bask or paint in. Although this half-acre garden was established when they arrived, Pat and Dave have blended their passions to add their own creative touches: a sunflower sculpture here, staddle stones there and a cobbled path made with reclaimed pebbles from the bubbling brook below the house. Intricate borders, a rare sequoia, a 200-year-old oak tree and local rare species of apple trees delight the eye while the sweet scent of roses, clematis, jasmine and passion flower perfume the air; children from the local school arrive once a year to crush apples and revel in the excitement of producing their own apple juice. A pair of greater spotted woodpeckers rear their young and tawny owls nest in the beech trees. You are encouraged to help yourself to bounteous vegetables: step out through French windows onto the glass-covered veranda with its scented climbers, picnic on the lawn, soak up the ambience.

Details

- Rooms: Self-catered studio for 2.
- Price: £70. £275-£420 p.w.
- Meals: Pub/restaurant 2 miles.

On your doorstep
- Black-a-tor Copse: ancient oak woodland, good year-round for lichens & mosses
- Lydford Gorge: lush, steep-banked river fringed with wild garlic in spring & fungi in autumn

Top tip
Take time to relax – & enjoy your own garden

Contact

Pat & Dave Woodhouse
The Annexe, St Raphael,
Mary Tavy,
Tavistock PL19 9PR

01822 810439
st_raphael@hotmail.co.uk
www.straphaelaccommodation.co.uk

Map: see page 14

The Old Rectory Hotel

Three natural acres of old rectory garden, with a pond & tumbling stream

The house

A rollercoaster lane sweeps you through woods clinging to the hill with the sea below: wash up at The Old Rectory to find peace, quiet, warmth, style. Friendly Huw and Sam, corporate escapees, have put their elegant mark on the place: uncluttered interiors and a pretty conservatory with an ancient vine whose grapes may appear on your plate. Find books, an open fire and bedrooms with big beds, crisp linen, cool colours; one has a balcony, most have super-cool bathrooms. Spin into the restaurant for an excellent meal, perhaps local asparagus, Exmoor pork, bread and butter pudding.

The garden

Sam and Huw took on a garden so overgrown that much of its structure was hidden; the joy of finding old paths, beautiful walls and borders has inspired them to keep going and create something magical for the future. About three acres in total, the garden sits snug in a natural hollow protected from the sea air and with Hollow Brook stream tumbling through it in a series of waterfalls, to land in a Victorian pond. Close to the house are a maze of rooms defined by restored herringbone walls: an old kitchen garden, now bustling with herbs and salad for the kitchen, a clipped box maze, and structured borders planted for colour, structure and scent. There are swathes of neat lawn, a pond with a bridge and an old sundial. Sam and Huw work hard to achieve a garden that is definitely not twee and blends easily into the landscape right on the edge of Exmoor. One hundred and forty-seven trees sway in the garden, including yew, copper beech, birch and larch; a glade of Himalayan silver birch trees is planned, to be underplanted with bluebells and wild garlic. Nature lovers will be happy here: enjoy a drink on the wooden deck overlooking the sea, and dream with the birds.

Details

- Rooms: 3 doubles, 4 twins/doubles, 3 suites.
- Price: £150. Suites £180-£190. Half-board £100-£130 p.p.
- Meals: Dinner, 4 courses, £35.
- Travel Club offer: Bottle of wine with dinner on first night for stays of 2 or more nights.

On your doorstep
- Marwood Hill Garden: National Collections of astilbes, tulbaghia, and – finest in June/July – Japanese iris
- Arlington Court House & Gardens: the damp, mild climate is perfect for rhododendrons & hydrangeas

Top tip
For a natural look, plant bulbs in clumps of 5, 7 or 9!

Contact

Huw Rees & Sam Prosser
The Old Rectory Hotel,
Martinhoe, Parracombe,
Barnstaple EX31 4QT

01598 763368
info@oldrectoryhotel.co.uk
www.oldrectoryhotel.co.uk

Map: see page 14

The Priory

An acre's worth of historic &
native planting

The house

It's beside the main street in the village – but the full impact of this stunning house doesn't hit you until you are inside. Dating from 1154 it was originally an Augustine priory; now Dawn has swept through with a fresh broom while keeping all the lovely architectural features; there's a 30-foot well in the drawing room. Bedrooms are spoiling and peaceful with deep mattresses on large beds with organic cotton sheets, herbs and fresh flowers; bathrooms are sumptuous. Dawn runs courses in textiles, food history and gardens. You are incredibly well looked after here.

The garden

Dawn calls the Priory gardens Luffendlic Stede, which means 'lovely place' in Old English. It extends to about an acre around the house, then slopes gently down to the village pond. Romance is definitely the theme in the 'hortus conclusus', a medieval courtly love garden with a turf seat, enclosed by a chestnut trellis covered in roses and old herbs. At the front, Dawn has planted three Tudor knot gardens; at the back, an apothecary's garden with a rose cloister and a replica medieval font with slate rills, surrounded by deep beds planted with scented flowers – roses, lavender, honeysuckle and lilies. The Textile Garden is filled with plants connected to either the designs on tapestries and embroideries, or the dyes, fibres and tools used to produce them. The orchard is being planted with old varieties of fruit trees (Devonshire Quarrenden, Court Pendu Plat) underplanted with wildflowers, and the raised vegetable beds are a celebration of organic companion planting. Three hundred native trees and plants have been planted in the first season alone, including willow, hazel, black poplar and limes. Wildlife includes kingfishers, bats and woodpeckers. A garden full of promise. *Open for pre-booked group tours.*

Details

- Rooms: 2 doubles.
- Price: From £150 for 2+ nights.
- Meals: Light supper, 2 courses, £25. Dinner, 4 courses, £40. Restaurant 8 miles.
- Travel Club offer: 10% off stays Mon-Thurs or bottle of wine with dinner on first night.

On your doorstep
- Grand Western Canal: the Devon section is a country park with great walks
- Knightshayes: rare shrubs & a Victorian walled garden, terraces & a round pond

Top tip
Plant native species to attract butterflies, birds & bees

Contact

Dawn Riggs
The Priory,
Halberton EX16 7AF

01884 821234
dawn@theprioryhalberton.co.uk
www.theprioryhalberton.co.uk

Map: see page 14

Higher Melcombe Manor

A two-acre cottage garden in a glorious setting

The house

You will thrill to this manor house of local stone, some of whose rooms date back to 1570. The sitting room has mullioned windows, the Great Hall has two stained glass windows, the dining room a log fire and long table. One bedroom is traditional with panelling, rich fabrics, grand stone fireplace and a bathroom along the corridor; leap into the 21st century above, where two rooms have plenty of pizzaz and a little sitting room between them. Lorel and Michael are still working on this huge inherited project, and are the most delightful people. *Smoking allowed in parts of the house.*

The garden

Come for the far-reaching views over Blackmore Vale towards Somerset: these two acres appear to blend quite effortlessly into the countryside, and Highland cattle are sometimes seen grazing in the pastures. At the front of the house there are sweeping lawns, a shrubbery woodland area and a deep herbaceous bank, its flowers tumbling over each other in waves of yellow rudbeckia, white stocks and pink sedums. Stroll along paths through the glade, where the dappled shade of an enormous copper beech creates the perfect spot for hellebores in spring and hemerocallis in summer; the tall blue spires of verbena soften the formality of clipped yew topiary hedges and open lawns. To the west of the house are island beds crammed with goodies, including towering hollyhocks, purple eryngiums and pink peonies. Here is a hidden pond and fountain and more little paths, bordered by lavender, which lead to a south-facing wall covered with climbing roses, clematis, figs and vines. Near the entrance to the house and chapel Lorel is making changes and introducing some special scented roses. Benches are dotted about and there are seating areas to east and west for sunny mornings and spectacular sunsets. *NGS.*

Details		Contact

- Rooms: 3 doubles.
- Price: From £95. Singles from £75.
- Meals: Pub/restaurant 1.5 miles.

On your doorstep
- Dorset Gap: well-known beauty spot with super views – a wonderful walk whatever the weather
- Thomas Hardy's Cottage: charming cottage garden, splashed with colour from spring to autumn

Top tip
Fertilise thoroughly. Be sure to have a bench to sit on and enjoy the sunset!

Lorel Morton & Michael Woodhouse
Higher Melcombe Manor,
Melcombe Bingham DT2 7PB

01258 880251
07973 920119 (mobile)
lorel@lorelmorton.com
www.highermelcombemanor.co.uk

Map: see page 14

Lytchett Hard

Cottage style borders, a
Mediterranean terrace &
shimmering harbour views

The house

The house takes its name from the place where
fishermen brought their craft ashore, in the unspoilt
upper reaches of Poole harbour. The three guest
bedrooms all face south and make the most of the
main garden below and the views beyond. Elizabeth
and David's green fingers conjure up a mass of
home-grown produce as well as flowers –
vegetables, jams, herbs and fruit. Guests can linger in
the antique oak dining room, or breakfast on the
terrace on warm days; there are log fires and a
lovely, huggable pointer called Coco. *Min. two nights
at weekends & July/August.*

The garden

One fascinating acre adjoins a reeded inlet of Poole harbour plus their own SSSI where, if you're lucky, you'll spot a Dartford warbler among the gorse. The garden has been created from scratch over the past 30 years and carefully designed to make the most of the views over heathland – haunt of two species of lizard – and water. Liz is a trained horticulturist and she and David have capitalised on the mild weather here to grow tender plants; copious additions of compost and horse manure have improved the sandy soil. These tender treasures thrive gloriously and are unusually large – you're greeted by a huge phormium in the pretty entrance garden by the drive; the terrace is a stone and gravel Mediterranean garden. Acid-lovers are happy, so there are fine displays of camellias and rhododendrons among hosts of daffodil and tulips once the sweeps of snowdrops have finished. Three borders are colour-themed, each representing a wedding anniversary: silver, pearl and ruby. Play croquet on the large lawn, explore the private woodland where David has created winding paths, relax in the shade of the gazebo or in the warmth of the working conservatory, admire the many unusual plants, or simply sit back and enjoy that shimmering view. *RHS, charity events & plants for sale in aid of Dorset Wildlife Trust.*

Photographs © Andrew Collinson

Details	Contact

Details

- Rooms: 2 doubles, 1 twin.
- Price: £70-£90. Singles from £50.
- Meals: Pub 1 mile. Restaurants in Poole, 4 miles.

On your doorstep

- Kingston Lacy: Japanese cherry trees spectacular in spring
- The Jurassic Coast: wild walks, crashing surf & fossil beaches
- Compton Acres: historic gardens inspired by their creator's worldwide travels

Top tip

Have fun doing your garden: if you enjoy it, so will everyone else

Contact

David & Elizabeth Collinson
Lytchett Hard,
Beach Road, Upton,
Poole BH16 5NA

01202 622297
lytchetthard@ntlworld.com

Map: see page 14

Dorset

Sondela

Colour throughout the year & heaps of roses in June

The house

All is leafy and sedate, with tall pines and rhododendrons hiding large houses; a short drive sweeps you to a colonial-style bungalow smothered in roses. Glynda and Selwyn, warm and intelligent, have filled their lovely light home with antiques and artefacts from their years in South Africa. Guests have a sitting room in soft blues, with a stone fireplace and fresh flowers. Bedrooms are quiet (the double is bigger, more modern) with pure white cotton sheets and splashes of colour from bedspreads and cushions; breakfast is in a gracious dining room or on the patio in good weather.

The garden

Glynda (a textile artist) gets enormous pleasure from her garden. When she arrived in 1998 she found a fatsia and a lilac on an unkempt lawn – and some lovely large horsechestnuts which still act as a windbreak. About two thirds of an acre have now been bullied and pleaded into shape with the help of bag upon bag of compost, tons of leaf mould and the expert eye of Glynda's mother, whose passion for orchids fills one entire greenhouse (two others are for wintering tender African plants). Used to gardening in a subtropical climate, Glynda has had to work hard for year-round interest (firstly using hose pipes to get the shape of beds right, then running upstairs to look down on them!), but the results speak for themselves. Roses bloom in profusion as they tumble over trellises and fences; interspersed are heuchera 'Palace Purple', *Alchemilla mollis* and lavender. A pergola has been erected and is now clothed in clematis, as 'Paul's Himalayan Musk' and banksia roses provide delicious scent; and there's a vine with lovely white grapes. There are outdoor seats and benches for outdoor gazing and grazing; you can't miss the splendour of the wonderful grasses, or the water feature with its hydrangeas, hostas and ferns. *RHS*.

Details

- Rooms: 1 double, 1 twin.
- Price: From £70. Singles £50.
- Meals: Dinner by arrangement. Restaurant 5-minute walk.
- Travel Club offer: Bottle of wine in your room. Late checkout (12pm). Free pick-up from local bus/train station.

On your doorstep
- Exbury Gardens: home of the Rothschild collection of rhododendrons, camellias, azaleas
- Annalal's Gallery: tiny garden on three levels, dotted with sculptures & paintings, owned by two RA artists

Top tip
Keep three compost bins: for filling, maturing, & use on the garden

Contact

Glynda & Selwyn Morrison
Sondela,
20 Chewton Farm Road,
Highcliffe, Christchurch BH23 5QN

01425 270978
morglyn@hotmail.com
www.chewtonbedandbreakfast.com

Map: see page 14

The Old Priory

Stone walls, trained fruit trees & romantic planting offer pleasure & peace

The house

Ancient, rambling, beamed and flagstoned, Jane's 12th-century home is as much a haven for reflection and good company today as it was to the monastic community who once lived here. Both house and hostess are dignified, unpretentious and friendly; Jane adds her own special flair with artistic touches here and there, and books and dogs for company. Find funky Venetian-red walls in the low-ceilinged, time-worn living room with a stone 14th-century fireplace and, in one bedroom, decorative wardrobe doors. The big bedroom – undulating oaken floor and four-poster – is deeply authentic.

48

The garden

Jane's bewitching walled garden in the beautiful Somerset town of Dunster is a wonderfully personal creation. You'll discover a bounteous blend of formal touches with shrubs, small trees and climbers which are allowed to express themselves freely. The garden perfectly complements her ancient priory home... a place of reflection, seclusion and peace. A tall mimosa greets you at the little gate on a lane overlooked by the Castle, mature espaliered fruit trees line the garden path and then comes Jane's most formal touch, the square, knee-high hedged box garden. The shrubs for this were rescued from the Castle's 'Dream Garden' when the National Trust abandoned it because they thought it would be too labour-consuming to maintain. Jane piled as many of the uprooted shrubs as she could into the back of a van, heeled them into some empty land and later arranged them into their present design. Informally planted herbaceous borders and a small lawn in front of the house complete the picture. Through an archway you wander into the church grounds with stunning long beds which Jane helps maintain. When the writer Simon Jenkins drew up his list of the best churches in England, Dunster received star billing and the grounds did even better. He described it as the most delightful church garden in England... see if you agree.

Details

- Rooms: 2 doubles, 1 twin.
- Price: £85-£95.
  Singles by arrangement.
- Meals: Pubs/restaurants 5-min walk.
- Travel Club offer: Free pick-up from Dunster station. Jar of Exmoor honey & free-range eggs (when available).
- Ethical Collection: Food. See page 10.

On your doorstep
- Dunster Castle: a subtropical paradise with strawberry trees bearing fruit in Oct/Nov
- Greencombe Gardens: a post-war organic garden; naturally and sympathetically planted collections

Top tip
Plant fruiting varieties of oriental blossom trees: for spring flowers, autumn fruit & winter shapes

Contact

Jane Forshaw
The Old Priory,
Priory Green,
Dunster TA24 6RY

01643 821540
www.theoldpriory-dunster.co.uk

Map: see page 14

Binham Grange

A garden that falls into the landscape & seduces all the senses

The house

Between the Quantock and Brendon hills, the coastal path nearby, Old Cleeve is an excellent area for walking. This place is perfect if you seek a bit of luxury when you haul your boots off. The stunning Jacobean manor house has been modernised with care: one bedroom is enormous with its own little sitting area and table for private breakfasts; both have super views, smart carpets, wind-up radios and rather posh bathrooms. Marie and her daughter Victoria are great cooks and all food is local, much is organic; you eat in what was probably the Great Hall, with a distant ceiling. Impressive.

The garden

Marie, a passionate gardener, has been involved with the restoration of Aberglasney Gardens, and she has created her own from scratch; about one-and-a-half acres around the house falling out into 300-acres of lush Somerset landscape. This garden has been planted to excite the senses and to enhance conditions for wildlife in an ecological way. There's a formal parterre to the east of the house, and a south-facing terrace which overlooks the cutting garden – a riot of colour from cosmos, nigella, calendula, roses, night-scented stocks and sweet peas. Beautiful organic vegetables are grown for the kitchen from Italian seeds; "to be a good cook you need a good garden," says Marie. To the west is the main terrace, a great spot to have afternoon tea or enjoy an evening drink while looking over the gardens to Exmoor and the West Somerset Steam Railway. Stroll round the part-walled garden with its pretty walls of red sandstone and blue lias, discover the orchard, look for otters in the river, watch the cows come across the field for milking... if you are lucky you will spot geese flying overhead. One guest described this as paradise. *NGS.*

Details		Contact
• Rooms: 1 double, 1 suite. • Price: £100–£140. Singles £80. • Meals: Dinner, 4 courses, £30. Restaurant 3 miles. • Travel Club offer: Complimentary tray of tea and cakes on arrival.	**On your doorstep** • Fyne Court: enchanting trails past folly & boathouse, bluebell copses & woodland garden • Exmoor National Park: wilderness, tranquillity & perhaps a glimpse of Exmoor ponies & wild red deer **Top tip** Save & plant your own seeds: cost-effective and rewarding! Start with nigella...	Marie Thomas Binham Grange, Old Cleeve, Minehead TA24 6HX 01984 640056 mariethomas@btconnect.com www.binhamgrange.co.uk Map: see page 14

Lower Farm

Two glorious acres of healthy
vegetables & salads for all seasons

The house

The Good Life in the depths of Somerset, and a
delightful family. The Dowdings have converted an
old stone barn into a self-contained apartment with
limewashed walls and lovely bedrooms with views.
It is perfect for families or a larger party: the cosy
oak-floored sitting room comes with a wood-burner,
a long wooden table and a sofabed. The whole place
has a charmingly French feel and Susie leaves you
breakfasts of homemade apple juice and granola
with organic yogurt, local bacon, eggs from their
happy hens and home-baked spelt bread, for you to
take at your own pace. *Min. two nights.*

The garden

Four generations of Charles's family have cared for and worked this land. Apricots soak up the sun on old farmyard walls, Sweet Heart melons lie heavy in the hand, a blossom-laden catalpa tree gently sways, children and pets roam free. Charles, a pioneering and passionate organic grower, has practised the no-dig method for 25 years, started one of the first veg box schemes in England and has written two books on organic growing. The glorious two-acre vegetable patch (scratched out of a paddock 13 years ago and gradually expanding to take in more of the field), two polytunnels and a hand-built greenhouse produce year-round award-winning salad leaves that travel not much further than five miles from the farm; this is very much a working garden. The rich, glossy palette of greenish-purple salad leaves form the backdrop to Susie's pretty decorative border in front of the barn, the 'cottage-garden' beds crammed with colourful favourites in the yard and the sweet-smelling rose and herb beds near the kitchen. Charles and Susie lovingly tend their plants, make preserves, run courses on veg growing, sort out the family and somehow manage to cheerfully greet and look after guests. An enviable life, but they have worked harder than we can imagine to create it. *Annual open day, otherwise parties by arrangement. Courses monthly.*

Details

- Rooms: 1 double, 1 twin, 1 sofabed.
- Price: From £90. Sofabed £45.
- Meals: Pub 0.5 miles.
- Ethical Collection: Environment; Food. See page 10.

On your doorstep
- Stourhead: 18th-century landscape garden, an extension of nature, with lake, grotto, turf bridge, rare trees & Palladian mansion attached; magnificent March daffodils & magnolias in May

Top tip
Grow plants without digging or disturbing: simply clear weeds & spread compost on top

Contact

Charles & Susie Dowding
Lower Farm,
Shepton Montague,
Wincanton BA9 8JG

01749 812253
enquiries@lowerfarm.org.uk
www.lowerfarm.org.uk

Map: see page 14

Pennard House

Informally landscaped garden with sweeping lawns & Victorian lake

The house

Pennard is incredibly grand in the don't-forget-to-pack-a-jumper way; it's been in Susie's family since the 17th century – the cellars date from then and the superstructure is stately, lofty and Georgian. You have the run of the library, drawing room, magnificent billiard room, 60-acre orchard, meadows, woods, and grass tennis court. Bedrooms have a mix of 'princess and the pea' style beds with mattresses to match, but all are very large with wide views, gorgeous linen, antique furniture and interesting pictures. Great for groups; it's a big house but still feels comfortably lived in.

The garden

Sweeping lawns, mature trees, a 14th-century church below, a south-facing suntrap terrace, a formal rose garden, pools and curious topiary... Pennard House is one of those dreamy landscape gardens straight from the pages of P G Wodehouse. All seems serene, graceful, easy – and on a grand scale – yet a huge amount of time and hard work has gone into developing and restoring the grounds of Susie's family home. Shady laurels and yews were the dominant feature until the couple launched a clearance and restoration campaign after taking advice from expert friends. Pennard House has, in fact, two gardens within a garden, divided by a little lane. There are the open, sunny lawns of the house garden and, across the road, a second garden with clipped hedges, a formal rose garden and that inviting spring-fed pool which in turn feeds a series of ponds below. Don't miss the witty topiary cottage, rabbit and other creatures which the gardener has created over the years. A recent success was ripping out cotoneaster below the terrace and replacing it with a formally planted combination of rosemary, roses and lavender. Knock a few balls around on the grass court, swim in the crystal clear water of the pool, or simply stroll among the scents and the blooms. *Open garden for local charity.*

Details

- Rooms: 1 double, 2 twins, 1 twin/double.
- Price: £90. Singles from £45.
- Meals: Pub 2 miles.
- Travel Club offer: Free pick-up from local bus/train station.

On your doorstep
- East Lambrook Manor: a prime example of the English cottage garden, designed by Margery Fish
- Avalon Vineyard: fine organic wines & rustic Somerset cider
- Glastonbury Tor: Somerset Levels views from the blustery top

Top tip
Plant garlic around roses to deter pests

Contact

Martin & Susie Dearden
Pennard House,
East Pennard,
Shepton Mallet BA4 6TP

01749 860266
07770 751357 (mobile)
susie@pennardhouse.com

Map: see page 14

Harptree Court

Delightful grounds landscaped in 1797 with a wide variety of trees

The house

Linda has softened this rambling 1790 house; it has an upbeat elegance. The rooms are sunny and sparkling with beds and windows dressed in delicate fabrics in fine contrast to solid antique pieces. On one side of the soaring Georgian windows are 17 acres of parkland with ponds; on the other, the log-fired guest sitting room and extravagant bedrooms. An excellent breakfast sets you up to walk the grounds and explore the garden. One condition of Linda's moving to her husband Charles's family home was that she should be warm! She is, and you will be, too. Relaxing and easy.

The garden

Three generations of the family still work hard in the gardens here: Charles's mother Mary, 85, oversees all, and can often be seen cutting grass on her tractor. Charles and his son-in-law Adam, a trainee arborist, do the large maintenance on the mature trees and shrubs. There are 70 acres, of which some 17 acres are woods, lawns and gardens, including a two-acre walled garden. On about a quarter of this grow vegetables, soft fruits and cutting flowers for the house; the rest is cultivated by an informal village co-operative. The two main lawns provide places to sit, read a book or play croquet; from the North Lawn you can plunge into woodlands with 200-year-old trees. Look further and you find more: folly, underground passage, ice house, waterfall, ha-ha, a lake with an island and clapper bridge... and a quarter mile of daffodils. From the South Lawn with its sculptural trees, a drive encourages a stroll towards a tranquil lily pond, a small fountain, a bench for pondering and an avenue of pleached limes. There are climbing roses against the boundary wall, a fragrant, paved garden created by Penelope Hobhouse, and some unusual trees including a catalpa, a tulip tree and a Wellingtonia. Come for teas on the lawn and peace, perfect peace. *NGS*.

Details

- Rooms: 3 doubles, 1 twin/double.
- Price: £95–£120.
- Meals: Pub 300 yards.
- Travel Club offer: Free airport parking and pick-up from airport.
- Ethical Collection: Community; Food. See page 10.

On your doorstep
- Milton Lodge Garden: a secret combe close to the city of Wells; explore a series of terraces with splendid views across the Vale of Avalon

Top tip
Make a slug barrier around vegetables with old coffee grounds – but not too close!

Contact

Linda Hill
Harptree Court,
East Harptree, Bristol BS40 6AA

01761 221729
07970 165576 (mobile)
bandb@harptreecourt.co.uk
www.harptreecourt.co.uk

Map: see page 14

Bristol

21 Royal York Crescent

A small, green, urban haven

The house

A large, airy and comfortable apartment on the promenade level of this gracious Georgian terrace – a perfect launch pad for all that the city has to offer. Susan is a relaxed and generous hostess, whose big, rosy-red sitting room with huge views to the Somerset hills is crammed with books, pictures and good furniture; meals are taken at a long table. The guest bedroom, with sparkling bathroom, is down the corridor at the back; wonderfully private, painted in creams and greens with pretty curtains of sprigged arbutus, it has doors to the delightful garden. *Min. two nights at weekends.*

The garden

Susan's former town garden was regularly open to the public under the National Gardens Scheme. Several years ago she embarked on a new project and her exotic little oasis flourishes: brick-edged beds on either side around a central courtyard theme, backed by high walls with plenty of colourful climbers such as *R. banksiae* 'Lutea', *Campsis grandiflora* and white jasmine. Large limestone flags set into gravel, with plenty of seating, lend interest, and a wooden clamber-entwined pergola gives height. This is a south-west facing garden and the big beds contain a mix of architectural plants, including a vigorous fig and a quince tree. Several attractive modern sculptures set in among them fit in well with this design-led space; a cube of 'floating stones' settles into a plinth of box and a ceramic pod is half hidden by choisya. A large ivy-covered water tank is set against a wall that supports an abstract triptych in bright blue – yet another place to linger and breathe in the peaceful serenity. It's difficult to guess you are within walking distance of a busy city centre in this secluded little retreat.

Details

- Rooms: 1 double.
- Price: £75.
- Meals: Continental breakfast. Restaurant 5-minute walk.
- Travel Club offer: Bottle of wine on arrival – hopefully to drink in the idyllic garden.

On your doorstep
- University of Bristol Botanic Garden: worth a visit for rare flora unique to the ecosystem of the Avon Gorge, e.g. the Bristol onion, Bristol whitebeam & spiked speedwell; the Gorge is a walk away

Top tip
Study local weeds & wildflowers & choose related plants for your garden to flourish

Contact

Susan Moore
21 Royal York Crescent,
Clifton,
Bristol BS8 4JX

0117 973 4405
mooresg@blueyonder.co.uk

Map: see page 14

The Bath Priory Hotel, Restaurant & Spa

Three innovative acres of kitchen garden, borders & magnificent trees

The house

Hotel heaven: everything is exquisite. Staff welcome you by name, the drawing room doubles as an art gallery, beds are turned down while you're at dinner. Burn off a few calories in the spa (pool, steam room, sauna, gym and treatments), then return for something ambrosial from the award-winning kitchen. Bedrooms are matchless, with rich fabrics, warm colours, fine wallpaper, shelves of books. Those at the back overlook the garden. Bathrooms are impeccable; one has fossils embedded in Jura stone. As for the city, stroll through the park to the Roman Baths and the Royal Crescent.

The garden

Head gardener and Chelsea Flower Show medal winner Jane Moore arrived seven years ago to a garden that had changed little since the 1930s: now these three acres burst to life with a croquet lawn, a walled kitchen garden, a stone terrace with a Mediterranean vibe and a heated pool. Settle into comfy wicker chairs and gaze out over a huge border filled with canna lilies and agapanthus. The garden is split in two and separated by an ancient stone wall; one side twists and turns with trees, secret spots, a meadow strewn with fritillaries, wild daffodils, cowslips, and a sunken pond ringed with David Austen roses. The other side is more Gertrude Jekyll: herbaceous borders, beds of interesting shrubs and a sheltered tropical spot; stray a little further into wilder areas to find gem-like flowers, woodland plants, hydrangeas and a glorious epimedium. This is a garden for all seasons: huge urns brim with bright orange and deep purple tulips in spring; lavender blooms all summer; bold dahlias and rudbeckias continue into autumn. A cedar of Lebanon holds court in the centre of the lawn, a rare Butan cypress is a treat and there are plans for a collection of flowering cherries. Jane propagates many of the plants you see here in her vintage greenhouse. Clever. *NGS, RHS.*

Details

- Rooms: 31 twins/doubles.
- Price: £270-£430. Suites £520-625.
- Meals: Lunch from £25.50.
  Dinner £68.50. Tasting menu £84.
- Travel Club offer: Drink on arrival (not Christmas or bank holidays).

On your doorstep
- Prior Park: serene valley park, with woodland walks, lakes & Palladian bridge with historic graffiti
- Hanham Court Gardens: visit in April/May for the snake's head fritillaries

Top tip
Scatter annuals (nigella, calendula) around young roses to plug the gaps while the roses grow

Contact

Sue Williams
The Bath Priory Hotel,
Restaurant & Spa,
Weston Road, Bath BA1 2XT

01225 331922
mail@thebathpriory.co.uk
www.thebathpriory.co.uk

Map: see page 14

Row Farm House

Semi-formal with old topiary: a peaceful retreat for lazy plant lovers

The house

A rare and ancient house in open rolling countryside. Discover stone mullions, leaded windows, original shutters with moonlight holes and a spiral oak staircase in a tower to the private, traditional bedrooms and a little reading room; views soar to Salisbury Plain and the White Horse. Cheerful Sara loves people and gives you Jersey-creamy breakfasts – in the garden on fine days. Musicians, thespians, bookworms, curious travellers and nature lovers will be beautifully soothed, Bath is a short hop for a concert or a play and the oldest inn in England is just over a mile away.

The garden

Fourteen years ago Sara arrived to a wild field of grass, a few trees and a glorious view of farmland. Borrowing Pliny's ideas, and using hidden lines and diagonals, she has made a garden with a narrow terrace by the house for sunny breakfasts, and a paved room over the road in the main garden with a Chinoiserie pagoda for lunch. There are plenty of corners for reading and talking, gates into her field and, behind the house, a herb- and rose-scented yard for an evening drink. You cross the garden through a series of gates, down the main axis to the final trompe l'oeil gate; the lawn is split by a path with a double row of yew and box topiaries, leading to a round trellis garden and another hidden path. To create mystery there are different textures of stone, grass, gravel, paving and trellising, and differing heights and widths of trees and shrubs. Planting is generous and natural: over 40 different clematis romp through shrubs and up walls, competing with roses – 'Mrs Herbert Stevens' and 'Variegata di Bologna' among others. Each border has a colour scheme and Sara raises lots of cuttings and bee-friendly species: there is a pretty raised vegetable garden and a little orchard leading to the beehives. The trees bounce with birds; silently watching are statues of the four seasons and some chubby putti. Lovely. *NGS, Wiltshire Gardens.*

Details		Contact
• Rooms: 1 twin, 1 single.	**On your doorstep**	Sara Jocelyn
• Price: From £100. Single from £50.	• Iford Manor: romantic Peto garden	Row Farm House,
• Meals: Pubs 1 mile.	in a steep valley; cypresses, summer	Laverton,
• Travel Club offer: A pint of cheering	opera & jazz	Bath BA2 7RA
Somerset cider on arrival.	• The Courts Garden: beautifully	
• Ethical Collection: Community;	eclectic garden rooms, topiary	01373 834778
Food. See page 10.	& arboretum	rowfarmlaverton@btinternet.com
	Top tip	
	Plant three climbers together to	Map: see page 14
	increase & prolong the flowering	
	effect	

The Mill House

Water meadows, wilderness garden & over 200 species of 'tree' roses

The house

In a tranquil village next to the river is a house surrounded by water meadows and wilderness garden. Roses ramble, marsh orchids bloom and butterflies shimmer. This 12-acre labour of love is the creation of ever-charming Diana and her son Michael. Their home, the time-worn 18th-century miller's house, is packed with country clutter – porcelain, foxes' brushes, ancestral photographs above the fire – while bedrooms are quaint and flowery, with firm comfy beds; organic breakfasts are served at small tables. Diana has lived here for many many years, and has been doing B&B for 27 of them!

The garden

The feel of family heritage in this house is perhaps most at evidence in the garden, which looms large within the passions of both Michael and Diana. Diana's love of gardening came from her mother, who taught her everything she knows. The whole garden spreads its rambling self over more than 12 acres, in which four 'rooms' predominate. Despite such a structure, wildlife and songbirds are the valued inhabitants of this alfresco extravaganza, who exist in and around the 200 species of roses, the old wooden summer house and the (weather dependent) water-filled ditch that divides the garden. Many of the apples, pears and tomatoes that will catch your eye find their way onto the breakfast table. The chalk stream flanking the garden harbours a Site of Special Scientific Interest and those in the know will instantly recognise the preconditions of a haven for butterflies and other environment rewarding species; the marsh orchids are a glory in May and June. The love of the owners for their own 'Garden of Eden' will no doubt enthuse any who cross the wide wooden bridge at its opening. If a garden can be a day's entertainment, then a couple of weeks may be required for this one. *NGS*.

Details		Contact
• Rooms: 3 doubles, 1 twin, 1 family room. • Price: £90. Singles from £65. • Meals: Pub 5-minute walk.	**On your doorstep** • Heale House: bordering the River Avon with a beautiful secluded Japanese water garden & spectacular summer colour • The Ridgeway: take in the wonderful views of open downland across Salisbury Plain	Diana Gifford Mead & Michael Mertens The Mill House, Berwick St James, Salisbury SP3 4TS 01722 790331 www.millhouse.org.uk
	Top tip For gardeners short of time: grow rambling roses rather than hybrids	Map: see page 14

Wiltshire

Durrington House

Old roses & peonies in borders, and a touch of sweet meadow & shingle

The house

You'll be well looked after in this pretty 1790 village house. There's a large, light sitting room with a grand piano you're welcome to play and an elegant dining room for breakfasts that include honey from a friend's bees, seasonal fruits from the garden and delicious kippers and local bacon. Bedrooms live up to their names, Lavender and Rose: each is charming with squishy beds and crisp cotton, masses of books to browse and views to garden or river. On warm evenings you can cool off in the outdoor pool, or stroll a mile and a half to Stonehenge. Salisbury is near for the dreamy Cathedral.

The garden

An enchanting little garden that surrounds the house on three sides and amounts to a third of an acre. Carole started from scratch and has created a proper English country garden in keeping with the house. Inheriting chalk soil she is restricted sometimes but prefers to work with, not against, nature; and she has triumphed. The main garden is walled with a semi-circular lawn immediately by the house, enclosed by a low beech hedge; this rises up a short slope furnished with limestone steps that lead to the upper lawn. Relax here at a black metal table, or eat under the shade of a tulip tree. Here too is a serene pool with a sunbathing patio, flanked by a hot border against the south-facing wall and a white-with-a-hint-of-pink border edged with box. A woodland area is more natural and produces a profusion of spring flowers, grasses and shrubs. Clever Carole, who, in her last house, designed an Elizabethan garden, has planted with a colour scheme in mind and looks for succession planting with interest in texture and scent, too. She takes her inspiration from books and visits to grand gardens.

Details

- Rooms: 2 doubles.
- Price: £75-£95. Single £55-£65.
- Meals: Dinner, by arrangement, £20. Packed lunch £7. Pub/restaurant 4 miles.
- Travel Club offer: Local food/produce in your room. Late checkout (12pm). Free pick-up from local bus/train station.

On your doorstep
- Heale House: eight glorious acres with carpets of aconites & snowdrops in Feb, a garden centre & lunches
- Chisenbury Priory: fine trees within clump & flint walls, billowing borders, mill leat, pond, orchard & wild garden. Pre-book

Top tip
A thick mulch is a back's best friend

Contact

Carole Lehman
Durrington House,
Church Street, Durrington SP4 8AL

01980 655405
07766 418904 (mobile)
carole.lehman@tiscali.co.uk
www.durringtonhouse.co.uk

Map: see page 14

Great Chalfield Manor

Alfred Parsons' Arts & Crafts garden perfectly complements the medieval manor

The house

A National Trust house – a rare example of the English medieval manor complete with 14th-century church and a family home where you will be treated as a guest not a visitor. Flagstones, a Great Hall with Flemish tapestries, perfect panelling, fine oak furniture and ancient elegance inspire awe – but Patsy dispels all formality with a gorgeous smile. Four-posters are swathed in the warmest colours, bathrooms are deeply old-fashioned and the only sound is bird ballad. Kitchen suppers follow large drinks in the prettiest sitting room. *Special two-night stays with local gardens tour.*

The garden

Stand in the middle of the lawn, close your eyes and imagine that Titania and Oberon have just fluttered past – open your eyes and they have. A structure of neatly clipped yew houses, upper and lower moats, herbaceous borders, huge lawns and an orchard have been immaculately tended and then enhanced by Patsy's love of soft colour and roses. The south-facing rose terrace brims over with scented pink roses that bloom all summer long, ramblers scrabble over anything with height, including old stone walls and the fruit trees in the orchard – and they are not alone; there is honeysuckle in abundance too, rambling hither and thither to waft its gorgeous English smell. Lavender and nepeta – the gentlest of hues – even the 'red border' is soft with smudgy colour, never garish. Water weaves through the grass in little streams which feed the serene moats and there is a magical woodland walk bursting with snowdrops in February. Patsy learned about gardening by "doing it" and gains ideas and inspiration from the tours she organised for 'The Garden Party' – but she has very firm ideas of her own especially when it comes to design and colour. There is a hazy, bloom-filled dreaminess about Great Chalfield. Perhaps Puck really does sprinkle something into your eyes as you go up the long, grassy drive... *NGS, Good Gardens Guide.*

Details		Contact
• Rooms: 2 doubles.	**On your doorstep**	Patsy Floyd
• Price: From £100. Singles from £80.	• The Courts Garden: delightful	Great Chalfield Manor,
• Meals: Supper £25.	English country gardens with tea	Melksham SN12 8NH
Pub/restaurant 1 mile.	room & plants for sale	
• Ethical Collection: Environment;	• Corsham Court: art-filled house	01225 782239
Community; Food. See page 10.	backed by park with lake views,	patsy@greatchalfield.co.uk
	majestic trees & folly, creation of	www.mingatgreatchalfield.co.uk
	'Capability' Brown	
	Top tip	Map: see page 14
	Cayenne pepper paste around young	
	tulip bulbs deters hungry voles	

Sheldon Manor

Deeply romantic, quintessentially
English gardens divided into 'rooms'

The house

Wiltshire's oldest inhabited manor house is a
beauty, Grade I-listed with a 13th-century porch
and a 15th-century chapel. In the renovated stable
yard are four soft-brick cottages with mullion
windows and sisal floors, fresh flowers and garden
views; elegant but not precious they are dreamy for
two... or one party together. Slip round the side to
The Wing with its stunning stained glass, big sofa
and wood-burner, and lovely beamed bedrooms
above. Play hide and seek in the blissful gardens,
take a dip in the romanesque pool. Seventy minutes
from London – heaven on the Cotswolds' fringe.

The garden

Discover a perfect, old-fashioned rose garden for summer and an arboretum of exotic trees for autumn: Caroline and Ken are committed to maintaining the plans laid down and executed so brilliantly by Major Martin Gibbs in the 1950s. There are eight acres here, charmingly divided into 'rooms': find newt-filled ponds, orchards bursting with plums, medlars, sloes and soft fruit, two ancient yews, a medieval grain store, lanterns strung between trees, a sunken garden, a potager for the house and a meadow, all joined together by stone walls and meandering paths. Roses cascade down walls and around windows, creating delicious scents in May and June; below the terrace is a wide path leading to a beautiful old stone love-seat. It is all deeply romantic and perfect for the bride and groom, and when there isn't a wedding you get it all to yourselves! Hunt for the Roman swimming pool with its imperious lion's head fountain, watch the coots and moorhens come to nest on the ponds, find the old wooden dovecote and the 1400s chapel, step out at dusk for the aerial display of bats. You can buy tree peony seedlings and divisions from old-fashioned rose shrubs and take a little bit of Sheldon home with you. *NGS*.

Details

- Rooms: 4 cottages: 1 for 2, 2 for 4, 1 for 6. Wing for 6.
- Price: £120.
- Meals: Pubs/restaurants 3 miles. Farm shop & café 1.5 miles.
- Travel Club offer: Welcome hamper of local, seasonal produce.

On your doorstep
- Lacock Abbey: woodland garden, Victorian rose garden & wonderful spring bulbs
- Westonbirt Arboretum: one of the most famous tree collections in the world – 17 miles of paths, glades & guided wildflower walks in spring

Top tip
Allow your garden & house to blend as one

Contact

Caroline Hawkins
Sheldon Manor,
Chippenham SN14 0RG

01249 653120
sheldonevents@btconnect.com
www.sheldonmanor.co.uk

Map: see page 14

Wiltshire

Ridleys Cheer

Fourteen acres: sublime in springtime, ravishing in June, fiery in October

The house

Rest your head on crisp cotton, wake to garden fruits and home-baked bread. The pretty house, in a peaceful hamlet down a meandering lane nine miles from Bath, was once a small cottage. Twenty years ago it was enlarged, one addition being the scented conservatory where you breakfast among oleander, jasmine and plumbago; new too is the spacious drawing room, inviting with log fires and books. Bedrooms, reached by a separate staircase, are light, airy and charming, with enticing garden views. Sue is an experienced Cordon Bleu chef; dinners, served at the mahogany table, are divine.

The garden

Plantsmen traditionally sacrifice design on the altar of collecting, but Antony and Sue combine both in a 14-acre garden packed with roses, wildflowers, rare shrubs and trees. Born gardeners, the Youngs began here modestly 40 years ago. In the lower and upper gardens, lawns sweep through displays including 120 different shrub and species roses, daphnes, tulip trees, a walnut grove and 15 different magnolias. The maturing arboretum contains a wide range of trees – beech, planes, hollies, manna ash, birch, 36 different oaks – through which roses cascade; broad mown rides radiate among acers in small glades. Serbian spruce were selected to attract goldcrests, which now nest here. Beyond is a three-acre wildflower meadow with 40 species of native limestone flora, a magnet for butterflies in June and July. By the house are touches of formality in potager and box garden, but the overall mood is of a profuse and breathtaking informality with glorious details and a ravishing collection of plants. Antony, garden designer and lecturer, wears his knowledge with engaging lightness. Students are sent here to learn about horticulture; plants are propagated for sale. Ridleys Cheer opens for the NGS and private groups. Exceptional. *NGS, RHS, Good Gardens Guide.*

Details		Contact

- Rooms: 2 doubles, 1 twin.
- Price: From £90. Singles £55.
- Meals: Lunch £20. Dinner, with wine, from £35. Pub 2 miles.
- Travel Club offer: A plant propagated from the garden: tree, shrub or herbaceous (wide range to choose from).
- Ethical Collection: Food. See page 10.

On your doorstep
- Dyrham Park: ancient deer park & garden in a gorgeous valley
- Bowood: a wonder of bluebells, rhododendrons & azaleas, in grounds landscaped by 'Capability' Brown

Top tip
Turn your fallen leaves into black gold: let them rot for 2 years until they are mulch

Sue & Antony Young
Ridleys Cheer,
Mountain Bower,
Chippenham SN14 7AJ

01225 891204
sueyoung@ridleyscheer.co.uk
www.ridleyscheer.co.uk

Map: see page 14

Cadwell Hill Barn

Lovely garden rooms hugged by ancient stone walls

The house

Elizabeth is a dynamo at interior design and gardens. The result: a stunningly converted barn wrapped in exuberant greenery and packed with interesting fabrics, paintings and handmade chandeliers. Arrive to tea and cake, or a drink in the raftered upstairs sitting room; downstairs, an open fire and Persian rugs create a cosy elegant feel. Bedrooms are soft calm spaces with comfortable beds and fluffy duvets; bathrooms have underfloor heating and walk-in showers. Countryside rolls into the distance, the village has a lively community and you're five minutes from the M4, yet quiet.

The garden

Pioneering Elizabeth revamped the house when she arrived 16 years ago, and, from a stone-strewn cattle yard, single-handedly designed and created the garden; it's the third garden to which she has added her magic. The result is a space hugged by ancient drystone walls, its distinct areas linked together by lush springy lawn and gravel walkways. The raised terrace, overlooking a circular Italianate garden (clipped box hedges, tidy topiary, a few sempervirens) is a delicious place to soak it all up. A mini maze and herbaceous border curl outwards and flow into the uninterrupted fields beyond; hedges of yew, beech and laurel reign supreme to protect delicate plants from strong southwesterly winds. Every tree you see, except for the line of pleached limes that stands solemn and magnificent behind the house, has been planted by her. The most unusual plant, a *Crambe cordifolia*, fizzes behind roped clematis and rambling roses; all summer the barn walls are veiled by Boston ivy and tubs burst with pretty flowers that may turn up in a vase in your bedroom. Guests are treated to the fruits (and vegetables) of all this labour – runner beans, salad leaves, tomatoes, blackcurrants and redcurrants. Delightful.

Details

- Rooms: 2 doubles, 2 singles.
- Price: £80–£100. Singles £50.
- Meals: Pub/restaurant 2 miles.

On your doorstep
- Westonbirt Arboretum: 600 acres of pathways & rare trees blaze with autumn colour
- Dyrham Park: very fine 18th-century house in rolling parkland with deer & a garden open in summer; great Tracker Packs for children

Top tip
For instant screening, plant a row of pre-grown pleached limes

Contact

Elizabeth Edwards
Cadwell Hill Barn,
West Littleton,
Chippenham SN14 8JE

01225 891122
maesdewi@uk2.net
www.cadwellhillbarn.co.uk

Map: see page 14

St James's Grange

A tranquil field-side garden for all seasons – with touches of formality

The house

In a pretty South Cotswold hamlet, next to a Norman church, is a sympathetic barn conversion and serenely comfortable home. Carolyn, well-travelled and great fun, welcomes you with homemade cake in the drawing room or suntrap courtyard. The smart light-filled double bedroom has passion-flower curtains framing the terraced garden view, the others overlook grazing sheep. Elegant furniture, horsey prints, fresh flowers, and not a murmur from the M4. Castle Combe is handy for an evening stroll, pubs in pretty villages abound. It's delightful. *Children over six welcome.*

The garden

A thoroughly pleasing mix of garden influences here: French and English-cottage, and a touch of Elizabethan formality. Carolyn enjoys trying out new ideas as the garden evolves from the field they started with. David has made a grand job of the drystone walling that borders the terrace (perfect for summer breakfasts) and the small croquet lawn edged with pleached limes (underplanted with chionodoxa and geraniums) and box parterres. There's a thriving walled kitchen garden tucked in by fruit trees and a copse effect of indigenous trees: effectively a windbreak beyond the beech hedging that encircles the sundial with its lavender surround. The courtyard area to the south of the house is a real sun trap: the raised beds are planted in whites, silvers, pinks, purples and blues echoed by wisteria, honeysuckle, clematis and the pink-flushed 'Phyllis Bide' rambling on the house walls. Terracotta pots at the kitchen door tumble with geraniums and herbs, water gently burbles within a stone urn. It's all so peaceful that partridges nest in the wild garden areas... tiny chicks can sometimes be seen following mum across the lawn. *NGS.*

Details		Contact
• Rooms: 1 double, 1 twin/double, 1 twin. • Price: £60-£70. Singles from £40. • Meals: Pubs 2 miles.	**On your doorstep** • Derry Watkins Special Plants: gardening courses & unusual plants for sale in exquisite valley setting • West Littleton: bluebells in the hedgerows April/May, and village gardens open May/June **Top tip** String unwanted CDs around soft fruit to keep birds away	Carolyn & David Adams St James's Grange, West Littleton, Chippenham SN14 8JE 01225 891100 dandcadams@stjamesgrange.com www.stjamesgrange.com Map: see page 14

Drakestone House

Formally informal – an Edwardian garden with a Mediterranean feel

The house

A treat by anyone's reckoning. Hugh and Crystal are utterly delightful people with wide-ranging interests (ex-British Council and college lecturing; arts, travel, gardening) and live in a manor-type house full of beautiful furniture. The house was born of the Arts and Crafts movement: wooden panels painted green, a log-fired drawing room for guests – wonderfully cosy – handsome old furniture, comfortable proportions, good beds with proper blankets. Drakestone House is elegant but human, refined but easy – and the views stretch to the Severn Estuary and Wales.

The garden

The hauntingly atmospheric Edwardian landscaped grounds would make a perfect setting for open-air Shakespeare – rather apposite since it's said that young Shakespeare roamed the hills around Stinchcombe. Hugh's grandparents laid out the grounds, influenced by a love of Italian gardens and admiration for Gertrude Jekyll. When Hugh and Crystal moved here, the garden was distressed and needed attention, particularly the magnificent topiary. The beautifully varied, lofty, sculptural yew and box hedges, domes and busbies dominating the view from the house are restored to perfection, creating a series of garden rooms with a backdrop of woodland. Paths and a romantic Irish yew walk invite you to wander as you move from one compartment to the next. By the house, a pergola is covered with wisteria in spring and rambling roses in summer, near displays of lovely old roses underplanted with lavender. Crystal describes these two acres as informally formal or formally informal – she can't quite decide which. But it's that elegant Edwardian design with its Mediterranean mood that makes Drakestone House so special. The best moments to enjoy the grounds are on sunny days when the shadows play strange tricks with the sculptured hedges and trees... expect Puck or Ariel to make a dramatic entrance at any moment!

Details		Contact
• Rooms: 1 double, 1 twin/double, 1 twin. • Price: £88. Singles £50. • Meals: Dinner £35. BYO. Pub/restaurant under 1 mile.	**On your doorstep** • Newark Park: colourful 19th-century displays of spring & autumn cyclamen • Painswick Rococo Garden: glorious year-round • Owlpen: an atmospheric Tudor mansion with a small formal garden **Top tip** If you want hardy, long-lived hedges, choose yew!	Hugh & Crystal Mildmay Drakestone House, Stinchcombe, Dursley GL11 6AS 01453 542140 Map: see page 14

Well Farm

An informal garden for all seasons, bursting with colour & variety

The house

Perhaps it's the gentle, unstuffy attitude of Kate and Edward. Or the position of the house with its glorious valley views. Whichever, you'll feel comforted and invigorated by your stay. It's a real family home and you get both a fresh pretty bedroom that feels very private and the use of a comfortable, book-filled sitting room opening to a pretty courtyard. Sleep soundly on the softest of pillows, wake to the deep peace of the countryside and the delicious prospect of eggs from their hens – plus local sausages and good bacon. The area teems with great walks.

The garden

Edward has a very good eye for scale and Kate has loved gardening since she was a child; she has made a garden wherever she has lived. This one has been the biggest challenge, plonked as it is on top of the windy Cotswolds with not a lot of soil. So the first thing they did was plant a mixed shelter belt of 1,000 trees. Now 20-foot high, it is doing a grand job and the garden is a delight. Bask in the south-facing courtyard, planted with cottage garden lovelies in neatly raised Cotswold stone beds, or wander down the lawn to admire the shrubs and old roses in the mixed borders; strike out further through a rose-covered arch to discover an orchard filled with traditional Gloucestershire fruit trees. The raised vegetable beds and the greenhouse are productive for months; gooseberries, red and black currants, damsons and plums may end up on your breakfast table and the brown speckled eggs are from the chickens by the tennis court (you may knock a few balls around if you like). A variety of unusual trees thrive in spite of the soil, birdwatchers will need to pack binoculars, there are benches and seats to watch it all from, and Stumpy the terrier is on rabbit patrol. Charming.

Details

- Rooms: 1 twin/double with sitting room.
- Price: From £80.
- Meals: Dinner from £20. Pubs nearby.

On your doorstep
- Rodmarton Manor: a heavenly garden all year, particularly at snowdrop time & in summer, when Rupert Golby's double herbaceous border comes into its own

Top tip
Kate's grandmother used to say, "a plant well planted is a plant half grown"

Contact

Kate & Edward Gordon Lennox
Well Farm,
Frampton Mansell,
Stroud GL6 8JB

01285 760651
kategl@btinternet.com
www.well-farm.co.uk

Map: see page 14

The Malt House

Quintessential Cotswold garden
planted to encourage tranquillity

The house

Two mellow cottages and a malt house combine to
create a delightful country hotel in the middle of a
village of sculpted golden stone. Inside, clipped
interiors are just the thing: parquet flooring,
sparkling wallpaper, fine fabrics at mullioned
windows, books, papers, an honesty bar and sofas by
the fire. Bedrooms are warmly elegant and hugely
comfortable, and breakfast is a feast: fresh fruit
salad, homemade granola, bread straight from the
oven, the full cooked works. All this and maps for
walkers, a list of local restaurants, hot water bottles
and umbrellas to keep you dry.

The garden

Right on the Cotswold Way, an impeccable three-acre English country garden runs behind the hotel and down to a stream, beyond which fruit trees (crab apple, plum, pear) are laden with bounty. Two herbaceous borders are a luxuriant mass of riotous colours: agapanthus, pink Japanese anemones, sedums and grasses; hanging baskets drip with well-tended flowers; roses climb walls and a smoke tree catches the eye. Equally impressive is Judi's kitchen garden: it provides freshly cut flowers for beautiful bedrooms and summer fruits and jams for breakfast. Guests are encouraged to help themselves to surplus produce and an American couple arrive every autumn to help with the harvest; the Turk's Head squashes were a huge hit last year. There's a thatched summerhouse overlooking the immaculate croquet lawn; pull up a Lloyd Loom chair for a G&T in the afternoon sun. Shooting off from the lawn, a semi-circular stone bench rests beneath an ageing oak tree; buddha heads perch in alcoves in the drystone wall and Caesar's bust can be glimpsed amongst the hostas. You are welcome to potter around the vintage greenhouse: it's home to experimental exotic vegetables, a huge fig tree, tomatoes, cucumbers and more. There are tons of walks and dreamy Hidcote Gardens are close.

Details

- Rooms: 2 doubles, 4 twins/doubles, 1 suite.
- Price: £120-£150. Suite from £160.
- Meals: Pub 200 yards. Dinner by arrangement (min. 12 guests).
- Travel Club offer: 25% off room rate on first night, Mon-Thurs.

On your doorstep
- Hidcote: a glory of wisteria in spring; interesting new varieties of fruit & vegetable are grown in the nurseries
- Kiftsgate: delicious variety of peonies in addition to the famous roses

Top tip
Keep lawn edges trimmed, then the whole garden looks tidy

Contact

Judi Wilkes
The Malt House,
Broad Campden,
Chipping Campden GL55 6UU

01386 840295
info@malt-house.co.uk
www.malt-house.co.uk

Map: see page 14

Ivydene House

Two glorious acres of informal, field-flanked country garden

The house

A joy to arrive and a pleasure to stay, at this red-brick 1790s house a short hop from the Malvern Hills. Rosemary greets guests with tea and homemade cake by the fire, Teddie (white and fluffy) shows you around the garden. Downstairs has been decorated in warm farmhouse style: old polished quarry tiles, cream walls, fresh flowers, wicker dining chairs, a great big inglenook. Fabulous bedrooms have an upbeat elegance with contemporary headboards – "just heavenly," say readers. Bathrooms sparkle, breakfasts are beautiful and Peter and Rosemary couldn't be nicer. Such value.

The garden

When Rosemary and Peter arrived some years ago they inherited a two-acre expanse of mud, weeds, stones and rubble. Since then everything, apart from a pretty sprinkling of old apple trees, has been planned and planted by the Gallaghers. Flanked on two sides by farmland, divided by a vast shrub-filled island bed, this garden is gorgeously, unpreciously informal. The most formal part is to one side – huge bed, pristine lavender walk, smooth lawn and yew-hedge archway leading to a pond with a water feature and pergola. The pond is surrounded by water-loving plants and is left alone to encourage wildlife – rest awhile and watch the moorhens flit in and out of the rushes. Or take a picnic and a rug to the lawn. Interesting trees like robinia, elder and eucalyptus are dotted about, and there's a pretty row of hydrangea 'Annabel'. The wilder other side of the garden is where mown paths swoop through a wood of 300 English trees, surrounded by a hawthorn hedge and with a trampoline in the middle. The lovely south-facing terrace with a Mediterranean feel has more seating areas; a sunny conservatory hugs the house. This is a young garden worth emulating – for its easy informality and its subtle, country-garden colours.

Details

- Rooms: 1 double, 1 twin/double.
- Price: From £75. Singles from £55.
- Meals: Pub half a mile.
- Travel Club offer: Drinks tray in sitting room. Selection of DVDs in bedrooms.
- Use your Sawday's Gift Card here.

On your doorstep
- The Malverns: stunning views of England's oldest hills – beautiful in all seasons
- Croome Park: 'Capability' Brown's first complete design, a peaceful landscape with year-round interest

Top tip
Always make time to enjoy your garden – just sit & admire!

Contact

Rosemary Gallagher
Ivydene House,
Uckinghall, Tewkesbury GL20 6ES

01684 592453
07879 463291 (mobile)
rosemary@ivydenehouse.net
www.ivydenehouse.net

Map: see page 14

Glanwye

Wye Valley gem mixes woodland, lawns, kitchen garden & borders

The house

Hugo was brought up here and even though he and smiley Henrietta throw open the house gladly to guests, it's still very much a family home. One bedroom with a carved four-poster has its own entrance and a comfy sitting room with lots of books and a mahogany table for delicious breakfasts, perfect for a romantic couple or those with a baby. The others are in the main body of the house, and all have good beds with antique linen, wash hand basins, proper blankets, plump eiderdowns, thick curtains and fresh flowers. Be independent or spoiled, it's up to you, but this is a super place to stay.

The garden

Mixing formal borders with terraced lawns, yew hedges, mature trees and rhododendron walks, the garden at Glanwye is the product of generations of care. Henrietta and Hugo are now custodians of this south-facing gem, surrounded by woodland and with stunning views of Aberedw Hill and the Wye Valley. At the bottom of the drive there's a large kitchen garden with box hedges, slate edges, a greenhouse with an ancient vine and productive peach, as well as a fecund orchard with cherry, apple and greengages. Spring starts with a mass of snowdrops under the pair of mature Wellingtonia by the house, then bobbing daffodils, camellias, enormous rhododendrons, an azalea path and a stunning walk through the bluebell wood. Sacks of tulips are planted each year in generous herbaceous borders, which, come summer, froth with delphiniums, plenty of old roses, *Alchemilla mollis* and anemones. The old lawn tennis court is a peaceful space surrounded by a mature yew hedge with a catalpa tree at its centre; a wildflower meadow blends seamlessly into the landscape and woodpeckers, kites and nuthatches are plentiful. Reg the Norwich terrier is happy to show you around. *NGS, RHS.*

Details

- Rooms: 5: 2 doubles, 1 twin; 2 doubles sharing private bath (let to same party only).
- Price: £70-£100.
- Meals: Pubs 5-minute drive.
- Travel Club offer: 10% off room rate Mon-Thurs. 10% off stays of 2 or more nights.

On your doorstep
- River Wye: fishing throughout the year & banks of wild daffodils in spring
- Tawryn: small, steeply terraced garden with oriental theme & long views to the Black Mountains

Top tip
Plant alliums like 'Globemaster' in a dormant acanthus bed for early season interest

Contact

Henrietta Kidston
Glanwye,
Hay Road,
Builth Wells LD2 3YP

07747 686041 (mobile)
henkidston@googlemail.com

Map: see page 14

The Old Vicarage

Informal shrubberies, lawns,
hidden places & exquisite views

The house

Blessed are those who enter... especially devotees of Victoriana. The house, designed by Sir George Gilbert Scott, is a delight. Your host, charming and fun, ushers you in to a rich confection of colours, dark wood and a lifetime's collecting: splendid brass beds, cast-iron radiators, porcelain loos, sumptuous bedspreads. Dine by candle or gas light (Paul cooks with panache), ring the servants' bell for early morning tea. You are on the English side of Offa's Dyke: look north to the heavenly Radnorshire hills, south to all of Herefordshire. *Min. two nights weekends & bank holidays.*

The garden

Hard to believe that only six years ago this garden had a complete overhaul. While Paul had a clear vision of the landscaping he wanted to create – rill, steps, waterfall, grotto, folly, dining terrace, sunken garden – he got expert advice about planting from designer Paul Cooper and it is now firmly established as a one-acre traditional garden with a mix of shrubs and trees, retaining much that was good about the old garden and melding exquisitely with the landscape and the church. The main lawn at the front has packed beds of perennials and plenty of seating by a rose and clematis arch; at the rear, the rill leads to a small waterfall over the grotto entrance. From here there is a cast-iron gate and a hidden staircase that takes you to the dining terrace with glorious views. In places lawns are left unmown to encourage spring flowers, there's a fecund camellia walk, swathes of hellebores, grasses, hostas, irises, euphorbias and day lilies. Here, old-fashioned roses thrive, alongside white wisteria and oodles of blue agapanthus; trees with interesting bark include white betula, *Prunus serrula* and *Acer griseum*, stunning in autumn. Paul is modest and talks about having luck, but his garden is a glory of birds, blossom, flowers and heavenly views.

Details		Contact
• Rooms: 2 doubles, 1 twin/double. • Price: From £98. • Meals: Dinner, 4 courses, £34. Pubs/restaurants 5-min drive. • Travel Club offer: 10% off stays of 2 or more nights (subject to availability).	**On your doorstep** • Bryan's Ground: a three-acre Edwardian garden, especially idyllic when iris sibirica 'Papillion' flowers in May **Top tip** Extend the seasons: plant miniature daffodils amongst hostas, & summer hyacinths amongst hellebores	Paul Gerrard The Old Vicarage, Norton, Presteigne LD8 2EN 01544 260038 paul@nortonoldvic.co.uk www.oldvicarage-nortonrads.co.uk Map: see page 14

Hen Dy, Nanhoron

Walled gardens & woodland
planted with passion over 250 years

The house

Hen Dy is the oldest house on the estate and was
the gardener's bothy and laundry, with a bell tower
that once announced mealtimes. Now you get a
sitting room, large, light and serene, with books,
games, soft sofas and Sky TV. The kitchen is made
for domestic goddesses, the smart dining room seats
eight, and in winter estate logs crackle. Up stairs –
or stairlift – to big restful bedrooms with garden
views. For ball games and barbecues you have your
own outside patch and you're surrounded by some
of the most gorgeous countryside in Gwynedd:
welcome to the Llyn peninsula.

The garden

People travel miles to see Nanhoron. The 5,000 acre estate has been in David's family for centuries; he and Bettina are delightful hosts and the gardens flourish on their watch. A baroque-inspired area set in a quadrant with topiary, statues and gazebo, with reflecting pool and views to lake, woodland and sea is the backdrop to your cottage. Steps take you to the lovely West Garden – part classic herbaceous border, part 'jungly' wilderness with huge rheums and bananas. A rose walk takes you to the East Garden: find ornamental vegetables and herbs and an orchard with 14 varieties of crab apple. Roses are everywhere – as are hydrangeas, camellias, azeleas and tree ferns; find them in abundance on the stunning woodland walk. Nanhoron is renowned for its fine trees, too: griselinia, a century-old ginkgo, sequoia, monkey puzzle, horse chestnut and centuries-old beeches. The river Horon meanders through the rolling parkland; listen out for the green woodpecker, spot a heron, and watch the pipistrelles at dusk. You benefit from home-grown veg and tomatoes, gluts of sweet things from the fruit cages and grapes from the greenhouse. The walled gardens, ablaze with their famous rhododendrons, are open until 6pm: this is heaven in May. *NGS, RHS. Open by appointment.*

Details

- Rooms: Self-catered house for 7.
- Price: £750-£1,200 per week.
- Meals: Restaurants 3 miles.
- Travel Club offer: Bottle of wine in your room.

On your doorstep
- Crûg Farm Plants: a wondrous cornucopia of exotic plants
- Bodnant Gardens: vast gardens lovely with camellias, magnolias & rhododendrons, berrying autumn trees & 100-foot-long laburnum arch; great views of Snowdonia

Top tip
Plant a tree & get a stick; plant a stick & get a tree!

Contact

Bettina Harden
Hen Dy, Nanhoron,
Pwllheli LL53 8DL

01758 730610
bettina.harden@farming.co.uk
www.nanhoronestate.co.uk

Map: see page 14

Golden Grove

Semi-formal Edwardian acres with topiary, terraces & ponds

The house

Huge, Elizabethan and intriguing, Golden Grove was built by Sir Edward Morgan in 1580. The Queen Anne staircase, oak panelling, faded fabrics and fine family pieces are enhanced by jewel-like colour schemes: rose-pink, indigo, aqua. In summer, the magnificent dining room is in use; in winter, the sitting room fire counters the draughts. The two Anns are charming and amusing, and breakfasts and dinners are delicious. They also find time for a nuttery and a sheep farm as well as their relaxed B&B. Many return to this historic, unusual, enchanting place.

The garden

The CADW Register of Landscapes, Parks & Gardens describes Golden Grove as "an attractive Edwardian terraced garden blending very well with the house, incorporating remains of a 17th-century walled garden". Walled on three sides, with terraces and steps sloping southwards from the house, these three acres are beautifully tended. A ha-ha has a large lawn below; a pleasure garden, nuttery and potager form three divisions. All the hedges and individual bushes of assorted sizes are yew, scrupulously trimmed in late summer and now allowed to grow to seven feet, firmly defining the different areas. The design is formal, with an emphasis on shrubbery and perennials rather than annual plantings, but colour is important and so is insect life; buddleia for butterflies and borage for bees. Plenty of mature trees and seating dotted about creates spaces for dreaming, perhaps by one of the two ornamental ponds, or through the ancient orchard; views are lovely over the surrounding beech woods. A substantial potager of raised beds produce oodles of organic vegetables and soft fruit; peppers and tomatoes jostle in the greenhouse. Through all this hum happy songbirds; you'll like it, too. *NGS, RHS.*

Details		Contact

- Rooms: 2 doubles, 1 twin.
- Price: £100. Singles £60.
- Meals: Dinner £30. Pubs 2 miles.

On your doorstep
- Bodrhyddan Hall: old walled kitchen garden, new picnic/forest walk & a Victorian parterre harmoniously replanted in summer
- Blaen Wern: a working dyer's garden; dye from 50 plants makes felted landscapes for the summerhouse

Top tip
Plant borage near your veg patch to encourage bees

Ann & Mervyn and Ann & Nigel Steele-Mortimer
Golden Grove,
Llanasa, Holywell CH8 9NA

01745 854452
golden.grove@lineone.net
www.golden-grove-estate.co.uk

Map: see page 14

Berkshire • Surrey • Isle of Wight • Sussex • Kent • London • Essex • Suffolk
Norfolk • Buckinghamshire • Oxfordshire • Warwickshire
Herefordshire • Worcestershire • Shropshire • Staffordshire • Leicestershire
Northamptonshire • Rutland • Lincolnshire • Nottinghamshire • Derbyshire • Cheshire

England: South East & Central

England: South East & Central

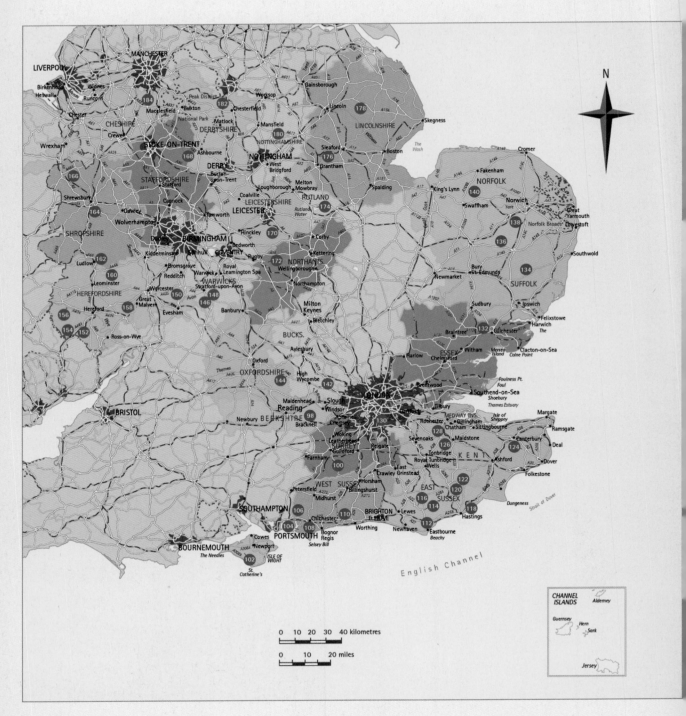

Special places to stay

Whitehouse Farm Cottage

Riotous cottage garden with a formal feel in a quarter of an acre

The house

Garden Cottage – 18th century, timber framed and gorgeous. The Old Forge is equally lovely; both are self-contained farm buildings in which you have complete independence and glorious views. And there's a lovely single room with its own sitting room in the 17th-century main house where Louise and Keir, film prop makers, live. The house and the cottages are filled with interesting objects and good antiques, beds are comfy and cotton is crisp. Overlooking farmland, this is a surprising find so near to bustling Bracknell – and a fabulous farm shop breakfast sets you up for exploring.

The garden

Only a quarter of an acre, but Louise and Keir have packed in so much interest with fabulous planting, it seems much larger. This enterprising couple took on an almost blank canvas in 1985 and have now created four 'rooms': the courtyard, the pond garden, the terrace and a circular seating area, all linked by pretty brick paths. To boost the serenity levels there are four water features: a natural pond, a circular 'pot' pond, a D-shaped lily pond and a small water feature with decorative metal fountain. Apart from the mixed traditional hedge round the pond garden (maple, ash, oak, hawthorn and holly) all the trees have been planted by Keir and Louise; a *Magnolia grandiflora* 'Maryland' is their pride and joy. Planting is gorgeously riotous: many climbing roses, honeysuckle, wisteria, solanum and plenty of herbaceous cottage favourites give colour and scent at the front of the house. At the back, many varieties of fern are happiest near the pond. Herbs also flourish and are used for cooking and tisanes. An army of hedgehogs, toads, frogs, slow worms and bats keeps slugs and snails at bay, while flitting birds happily redistribute seeds. A much-loved garden which you are welcome to wander through – and catch the seasonal surprises. *NGS*.

Photographs © Derek St Romaine

Details		Contact

• Rooms: 1 double, 1 suite,
  1 suite for 1.
• Price: £80-£100. Singles £70-£90.
• Meals: Pubs/restaurants 1 mile.
	On your doorstep
	• The Royal Landscape: 1,000 acres of
	  woodland, lakes & gardens,
	  meandering paths, plunging views
	  & a superb ornamental garden
	• Basildon Park: guided walks around
	  historic parkland – & bluebell
	  woods
	
	Top tip
	Order top-quality bulbs & seeds,
	and order them early
		Keir Lusby
		Whitehouse Farm Cottage,
		Murrell Hill Lane, Binfield,
		Bracknell RG42 4BY
		
		01344 423688
		07711 948889 (mobile)
		garden.cottages@ntlworld.com
		
		Map: see page 96

Nurscombe Farmhouse

Semi-formal, part-walled garden on several levels surrounded by hills

The house

It is blissfully peaceful. You enter through an old archway, past irises, hollyhocks and wooden gates, to discover a 15th-century farmhouse. Beautifully restored barns and stables are scattered around; sheep munch in the fields below. You can slump in front of a fire in the drawing room, sleep quietly in simple, characterful bedrooms with well-worn carpets, striped wallpaper and long views; frill-free bathrooms are in traditional working order. A proper farmhouse breakfast sets you up for a visit to the Norman church at Compton or a country walk. *Minimum stay two nights at weekends.*

The garden

No fewer than 36 leylandii trees had to be banished when Jane took over. Once they had gone, a garden, walled on three sides, was revealed. Since then she has worked steadily to achieve a true cottage-garden effect. Working on sandy soil, her aim is for it to look "casually cared for, not too formal". She has achieved this – brilliantly. A rose and vine-covered pergola is just outside the front door – a grand place to sit and gaze over the fields. A mixed herbaceous border behind the house has random repeat planting at either end. 'Iceberg' roses on a bargate wall provide a backdrop for a sloping border with a blue, pink and magenta colour scheme; at the back are *Crambe cordifolia* and pretty cranesbill. In the vegetable garden, where there's a fine old wooden greenhouse, a tayberry flourishes against the back wall and herbs, root vegetables, beans, courgettes and sugar snaps grow. Fruit from the old apple and plum trees sometimes appear on the breakfast menu, along with wild mushrooms and nuts. The garden, set in 40 acres of gentle hills (bluebell woods, a trout-filled lake, a rowing boat), is visited by birds and the occasional hedgehog, fox or badger.

Details

- Rooms: 1 double, 1 twin.
- Price: From £80. Singles from £45.
- Meals: Pub/restaurant 1 mile.

On your doorstep
- Loseley Park House: ancient wisteria, vine walks, roses & walled rooms; a delight in June/July
- Wisley: beautiful & practical RHS flagship garden; a vast greenhouse encloses rare delicate plants from warmer climes

Top tip
Cut back perennials hard after flowering & water when necessary

Contact

Jane Fairbank
Nurscombe Farmhouse,
Snowdenham Lane,
Bramley GU5 0DB

01483 892242
fairbank@onetel.com
www.nurscombe.com

Map: see page 96

Northcourt

Natural garden with 10,000 plants,
from herbs to maritime to exotics

The house

Think big and think Jacobean. Built in 1615 by
the deputy governor of the Isle of Wight, Northcourt
was once the manor house of a 2,000-acre estate.
Extensively modified in the 18th century, the
house has 80 rooms including a library housing a
full-sized snooker table (yes, you may use it), and a
32-foot music room (you may play the piano, too).
Bedrooms are large, in two separate wings, and
bathrooms great, but this is still a warm and
informal family home – and your hosts more than
likely to be found in gardening clothes. Autumn is
an excellent and less busy time to visit.

The garden

Northcourt's astonishing 15 acres have developed over the last four centuries into a garden of historical interest and a paradise for plantsmen. The Isle of Wight remains warm well into the autumn, and in its downland-sheltered position the garden exploits its microclimate to the full. Able to specialise in such exotics as bananas and echiums, the Harrisons have developed a sub-tropical garden; higher up the slope behind are Mediterranean terraces. There's extensive variety: the chalk stream surrounded with bog plants, the knot garden planted with herbs, the walled rose garden, the sunken garden, the one-acre kitchen garden, a Himalayan glade and a maritime area. All this represents a collection of 10,000 plants, some occasionally for sale – how do they do it? Modest John, the plantsman, says it is the good soil and atmosphere that allows everything to grow naturally and in profusion. But that is only half the story – he has left out the back-breakingly hard work and commitment that have gone into it. They are knowledgeable too – he is a leading light in the Isle of Wight Gardens Trust, Christine was once the NGS county organiser for the island. Between them they have done a huge amount to encourage horticultural excellence in the area. *NGS, RHS, Good Gardens Guide, Isle of Wight Gardens Trust.*

Details

- Rooms: 6 twins/doubles.
- Price: £65-£105.
  Singles £45-£57.50.
- Meals: Pub 3-minute walk through gardens.
- Travel Club offer: 15% off stays of 4 or more nights.

On your doorstep
- The Needles: take a wonderful walk to the island's famous landmark – & a bus back!
- Osbourne House: Queen Victoria's walled gardens & exotic hothouses, plus regal Solent views

Top tip
Grow plants that do not need staking or watering, & mulch well

Contact

John & Christine Harrison
Northcourt,
Shorwell PO30 3JG

01983 740415
07955 174699 (mobile)
christine@northcourt.info
www.northcourt.info

Map: see page 96

Church Gate

Lounge lizards enjoy this one-acre plot – as do wildlife & weeds!

The house

Janie has added a conservatory and a huge sunny Aga kitchen to her 1930s house; she greets with afternoon tea, rustles up tasty home eggs at breakfast, and may even treat you to home-baked bread or croissants, served on the terrace in summer. The house is adorned with Nigerian musical instruments and Janie's photographs; the bedrooms are fresh with low windows looking onto the garden. There are lovely soaps in the bathrooms and driftwood lamps in the flagstoned sitting room. Set off for nearby Chichester with its theatre and shops – or pretty Itchenor, a mecca for sailors.

The garden

Janie is a whizz in her one-acre plot, often to be seen toiling away in her boiler suit! She particularly loves highly scented flowers, interesting foliage and architectural plants for arranging in the house. The main jobs when they moved in were to take out the non-productive fruit trees and put in a few more, to plant trees and hedges (such as photinia 'Red Robin') for structure, and to create separate areas, all of which has softened some rather hard edges and hidden a somewhat peculiar earlier design to the front of the house. They are lucky in that the Manhood Peninsula seems to have its own very gentle microclimate, so losses of more tender plant varieties are rare. A new south-facing terrace outside the kitchen has a narrow rill which circulates from a small pond: a table here is lovely for outdoor eating, while an oak pergola covered with *Vitis vinifera* 'Phoenix' and *Wisteria sinensis* 'Caroline' provides shade. From here there are two large beds leading away from the house, planted up with feathery *Stipa gigantea* and elegant *Verbena bonariensis*. Janie has also planted some unusual trees including *Eucalyptus debeuzevillei*, *Podocarpus salignus* and *Cercis canadensis* 'Forest Pansy'.

Details

- Rooms: Cottage: 1 double, 1 twin with sitting room.
- Price: From £85. Singles from £65.
- Meals: Pub 4 miles.
- Travel Club offer: Bottle of wine in your room. Local food/produce in your room.
- Ethical Collection: Food. See page 10.

On your doorstep
- Pagham Harbour: tidal mudflats attract thousands of birds for the keen twitcher
- West Wittering Beach: walk from here to East Head Spit – a rare piece of untouched coastline

Top tip
Hedgehogs love slugs & insects: encourage by leaving a pile of twigs & leaves in a corner

Contact

Janie Impey
Church Gate,
Itchenor,
Chichester PO20 7DL

01243 514700
janie.allen@btinternet.com
www.chichesterbandb.co.uk

Map: see page 96

Lordington House

"What wondrous life is this I lead!"
– Andrew Marvell

The house

On a sunny slope of the Ems valley, life ticks by peacefully as it has always done... apart from a touch of turbulence in the 16th century. The house is vast and impressive, with majestic views past clipped yew and pillared gates to the AONB beyond. Inside is engagingly old-fashioned with a few quirky flare-ups like a hand-painted harlequin design in the hall. Find Edwardian beds with proper bedspreads, Sixties-style bathrooms, shepherdess wallpapers up and over wardrobe doors. Tea cosies at breakfast, big log fires and a panelled drawing room. Bring your woolly jumper! *Over fives welcome.*

The garden

The arrival is dramatic, a gentle rise, with – in spring – a sea of daffodils to either side; you slip between two stone pillars that appear to lean slightly outwards to allow you in. Emerge onto pea gravel in front of this truly beautiful house. The first impression of the garden is – bizarrely given its age – one of modernity; the crisp green wall of neatly sculpted golden yew and tall pines strike a contemporary note. Hedges and lawn live at the rear, rubbing shoulders with huge old stone walls and another pair of splendid gateposts which lead to the lime avenue, through which you may spot horses – bucolic bliss. A cherub waves from one wall and the view stretches effortlessly away. Long borders romp with low-growing aromatic shrubs, interspersed with pelargoniums, lilies, anemones and osteospermum. In the spring, the beds are bright with tulips; there are some old and interesting trees including a black mulberry and a paperbark maple. Well-behaved vegetables sit in their rows, hundreds of cuttings are reared annually in the greenhouses, there are lovely places to sit with a glass of wine and a good book, and – for real gardeners – Audrey will be a treat to talk to. Overhead, buzzards wheel and mew. *NGS*.

Details

- Rooms: 2 doubles, 1 twin/double, 1 single.
- Price: From £95. Singles from £47.50.
- Meals: Dinner £25. Packed lunch from £5. Pub 1 mile.
- Travel Club offer: Free pick-up from local pubs or stations.

On your doorstep
- West Dean: a husband & wife team care for these 90 acres; plus garden courses, chilli fiesta, restaurant & shop
- Kingley Vale: ancient twisted yews, superb chalk grassland, birds & butterflies galore

Top tip
Conkers make excellent mothballs; spiders hate them too

Contact

Mr & Mrs Hamilton
Lordington House,
Lordington,
Chichester PO18 9DX

01243 375862
hamiltonjanda@btinternet.com

Map: see page 96

Quay Quarters, Apuldram Manor Farm

A formal half-acre rose garden with a wonderful 50-foot pergola

The house

A working farm a short stroll from Chichester with four spotlessly converted cottages – all together but private. Old oak spans the ceilings, new oak the floors. Bedrooms are light and airy with deeply comfortable beds; all-white bathrooms have mosaic tiles and one has a corner bath and luxurious shower. In each cottage the space is uncluttered, the lighting subtle, the colours 'cool' and the heating underfloor. There are DVDs, books, games, stereo, too. Some have their own little terraces, all is utterly peaceful in this AONB. Great beaches at West Wittering are a few miles away.

The garden

Lorraine's mother-in-law began Apuldram Roses Nursery years ago, from the old stable block that is now Rose Cottage: they continue to trade and attend all the large flower shows. The old orchard was formally planted with all the rose varieties that were sold bare root or in pots, and a 50-foot pergola was added to showcase the climbers and ramblers – 'Albertine', 'Dorothy Perkins', 'Paul's Scarlet', 'Dublin Bay'. To add colour in spring, daffodils have been naturalised in the grass, the pergola is underplanted with lavender and clematis, and an early flowering 'Canary Bird' sits among the standard roses. Many of the borders are surrounded with box hedging and bay, and there's also a 30-foot high flint wall – a glory when the climbers come into bloom. A thuja hedge separates all this from Lorraine's private garden, which you are also welcome to wander: a series of elegant 'rooms' including a topiary garden, box balls, a formal vegetable plot, a winter-flowering clematis-covered arch, and gravel paths leading to an orchard. A 50-foot herbaceous border runs the length of the garden and is protected by a mixed hedge: a riot of chocolate cosmos, hollyhocks, lupins, penstemons and many other cottage favourites. Delightful.

Details

- Rooms: Self-catered cottages: 2 for 2, 1 for 4, 1 for 6.
- Price: £370-£1,000 per week.
- Meals: Pub half a mile.

On your doorstep
- West Dean: vast house, restored walled garden, 300-foot-long Edwardian pergola, spring garden & arboretum, open all year
- Denmans Gardens: a tamed wilderness of foliage & form, designed by John Brookes

Top tip
Use evergreen box & bay to give structure during the winter months

Contact

Lorraine Sawday
Quay Quarters,
Apuldram Manor Farm,
Dell Quay, Chichester PO20 7EF

01243 839900
cottages@quayquarters.co.uk
www.quayquarters.co.uk

Map: see page 96

Pindars

Almost an acre which, Topsylike, "just growed". Atmospheric & imaginative

The house

Jocelyne and Clive are excellent company and their 1960s house is warm, well-loved and lived-in. The road is there but the guest sitting room faces the beautiful gardens, as do two of the bedrooms; the other has distant views of Arundel Castle. Bedrooms are light and comfortable, cosy and compact; bathrooms are not state of the art, but white and pristine. Books, magazines, watercolours and two Burmese cats complete the happy picture. Jocelyne's cooking is imaginative, vegetables are home-grown, breakfast and dinner are delightful. Close to Goodwood. *Two nights preferred.*

The garden

The weeds towered above the children when Jocelyne and Clive bought the field 42 years ago. Once the house was built, they had £5 left for creating the garden – from scratch! Over the years, they have softened and transformed the square lines of the field into a magical place of curves and corners, open vistas and secret places. Everything – terraces, swimming pool, flint wall with fountain – has been designed and built by them. They have also planted about 100 trees, including poplars, birches, eucalyptus, oaks and cherries, some of which are felled as necessary. Jocelyne's particular love is the *Acer platanoides*, fully grown and superb; another special tree is a big chestnut, reared from a conker and nursed back to life by Clive after it was split in half by the 1987 gale. The borders are a mix of shrubs and perennials with some summer bedding (though she also fills pots with annuals, which she can then move around). She plants for foliage colour, shape and height in large, naturally shaped splodges. If plants seed themselves, they are often allowed to stay, giving a relaxed, unstudied effect. Ask about Doris, Constance and frigid Freida and Jocelyne will be happy to introduce you. *NGS, RHS. Open garden for various charities.*

Details

- Rooms: 2 doubles, 1 twin.
- Price: From £75. Singles from £45.
- Meals: Dinner (when possible) from £22. Pub/restaurant 0.5 miles.
- Travel Club offer: Glass of wine and selection of canapés at 6pm each evening of visit.
- Ethical Collection: Community; Food. See page 10.

On your doorstep
- Arundel Castle: the peach house shelters a cornucopia of exotic produce
- Parham House & Park: seven acres of Pleasure Grounds & four of walled gardens, a profusion of lilies & roses

Top tip
Plant alliums along with heuchera or geraniums to hide the alliums' dead leaves

Contact

Jocelyne & Clive Newman
Pindars,
Lyminster,
Arundel BN17 7QF

01903 882628
pindars@tiscali.co.uk
www.pindars.co.uk

Map: see page 96

Sussex

Ocklynge Manor

Two thirds of an acre of all-year-round interest & ancient walled garden

The house

On top of a peaceful hill, a short stroll from Eastbourne, is a tip-top B&B in an 18th-century house with an interesting history – ask Wendy! Here you are treated to home-baked bread and delicious tea time cakes and jams; on fine days you can take it all outside. Cream-carpeted, bright sunny bedrooms, all with views over the garden, create a mood of relaxed indulgence and are full of thoughtful touches: dressing gowns, DVDs, mini fridges. Breakfasts are superb and there's a chintzy, comfy sitting room just for guests. This is a very spoiling, very nurturing place.

The garden

The ancient walled garden was once wandered through by the Knights of St John of Jerusalem; you are just as welcome. Wendy has battled with poor topsoil on top of solid chalk rock, but, ten years on, has designed everything in her two thirds of an acre to be as easy to manage as possible. There is a pergola down the centre of the garden with rhododendrons and azaleas at the end, a small pond surrounded by bonsai trees, a little turret that used to be the look-out tower for the Eastbourne post and a 200-year-old rockery. The garden year starts with wild garlic bulbs, daffodils, bluebells and primulas; next come forget-me-nots and *Clematis montana* 'Rubra'. A Kiftsgate rose dominates an arch and has escaped up an ash tree, acid-lovers grow in oak tubs or terracotta pots. Mature trees include a very old manna ash, and a holm oak. The borders are filled with contrasting evergreen shapes and climbers growing into trees. The orchard contains apples, a pear, a fig and a small yellow cherry plum; a raised bank at the back is filled with the prettiest violets and cow parsley in the spring, and there are lots of benches at suitable spots from which to take it all in. *NGS.*

Details		Contact
• Rooms: 1 double, 1 twin, 1 suite for 3. • Price: £90. Singles from £50. • Meals: Pub 5-minute walk.	**On your doorstep** • Pashley Manor: 11 acres of quintessentially English landscaping, imaginative planting & fine old trees • Great Dixter: amazing bursts of exotic colours from the late, great Christopher Lloyd **Top tip** Pinch out the centre candle of pines when new growth appears	Wendy Dugdill Ocklynge Manor, Mill Road, Eastbourne BN21 2PG 01323 734121 07979 627172 (mobile) ocklyngemanor@hotmail.com www.ocklyngemanor.co.uk Map: see page 96

Hailsham Grange

An informally formal haven
beside the parish church

The house

Come for elegance and ease. Noel welcomes you
into his lovely Queen 'Mary Anne' home (a vicarage
built in 1701), back from the road next to the
church. No standing on ceremony here, despite the
décor: classic English touched with chinoiserie in
keeping with the house. Busts on pillars, swathes of
delicious chintz, books galore and bedrooms a treat;
the four-poster and the double overlooking the
garden share a sitting room. Summery breakfasts
are served on the flagged terrace, marmalades and
jams on a silver salver. The town garden with its box
parterre and flowers is an equal joy.

The garden

There is a quiet element of the unexpected in Noel's garden (featured in *Country Life* in 2010), which is as stunning as the house. Perhaps it's because of his upbringing in New Zealand, at a time when many gardens still clung to traditional English patterns but were enlivened by native exotics. Here, within a formal framework of box, yew and hornbeam hedging, Noel has created a whole series of gardens, yet within the formality, has mixed and juxtaposed his plants in an informal and original way. The effect is relaxed, romantic and subtly different. Separate areas are themed for colour – of foliage or flower – with plants chosen for scent and grouped in swathes so they blend into each other. All this has been achieved in the years since Noel took over Hailsham Grange. When he arrived, in 1988, he was presented with the challenge of a completely blank, one-acre canvas and is still constantly experimenting (the spring garden is where any plants that are doing badly are given their last chance – it's flourish or die!). There are several enticing spots to sit with an evening drink and contemplate all this beauty: a bench in the daffodil-filled spinney, a chair in the dell, and a seat in the enchanting gothic summerhouse. Look out for the unusual plectranthus! *NGS, Good Gardens Guide.*

Details		Contact
• Rooms: 2 doubles, 2 suites. • Price: £95-£120. Singles from £70. • Meals: Pub/restaurant 300 yards. • Use your Sawday's Gift Card here.	**On your doorstep** • Pashley Manor: exquisite English gardens with Tulip Festival showcasing 90 varieties & 20,000 blooms end April/May • Arlington Bluebell Walk & Farm Trails: dog-friendly too	Noel Thompson Hailsham Grange, Hailsham BN27 1BL 01323 844248 noel@hgrange.co.uk www.hailshamgrange.co.uk
	Top tip Water sparingly to help plants cope better with a dry spell	Map: see page 96

Sussex

Netherwood Lodge

English planting for colour,
shape & surprise

The house

The whiff of log fire, the scent of fresh flowers and a smattering of chintz over calm uncluttered interiors will please you in this single-storey, L-shaped coach house. Engaging Margaret may give you homemade cake or scones in an elegant sitting room with views over the garden, and cosy bedrooms are beautifully dressed and chic: wool carpets, silk and linen curtains, oak furniture – and gloriously comfortable beds. You eat well, too: much is locally sourced and breakfasts are flexible. This is a quiet part of East Sussex, ideal for walking, National Trust properties and Glyndebourne.

The garden

When Margaret moved into the house in 1986, this quarter acre of garden was totally overgrown. The planting, the rockery, the fruit trees, the York stone paths and the herbaceous beds have all been created since. Now she has a very private south-facing plot, surrounded by hedges and backing onto farmland and a wood where birdlife abounds. There are plenty of seating areas and benches for maximising time in the sun – or heading for cool shade; there's a rustic arch with a Kiftsgate rose, seasonal pots and large wooden barrels filled with shrubs and small trees. Planting is traditional and well thought out. Margaret is very house proud about her garden, takes lots of cuttings and buys only local plants; over 300 tulips burst into life in March and go all the way through to May. Scent is important – honeysuckles, lavenders – while roses and clematis provide height, structure and plenty of heavenly whiffs. Violas tumble out of window boxes, sweet peas out of baskets; geraniums, begonias and roses bloom throughout the summer in the exceptionally good soil here. In autumn the tints from the woodland are stunning. All year round it is deeply peaceful. *NGS.*

Details

- Rooms: 1 twin, 1 double.
- Price: From £100. Singles from £80.
- Meals: Pub/restaurant 1 mile.
- Travel Club offer: Local food/produce on your departure.
- Ethical Collection: Food. See page 10.

On your doorstep
- Bateman's: former home of Rudyard Kipling, with beautiful gardens & wildflower river meadow
- Sheffield Park: magnificent spring & autumn colours

Top tip
Be bold with colour (eg. pink & orange together) & avoid straight lines

Contact

Margaret Clarke
Netherwood Lodge,
Muddles Green, Chiddingly,
Lewes BN8 6HS

01825 872512
netherwoodlodge@hotmail.com
www.netherwoodlodge.co.uk

Map: see page 96

Knellstone House

Exuberance within boundaries
– and a veranda for views

The house

The Harlands have a stunning old house, built as a hall in 1490, with sloping, solid oak floors, mullioned windows and rare dragon beams. Glorious views reach across the Brede valley to sheep and then the sea. No old style interiors but a refreshingly modern and bright feel with buttermilk walls, contemporary furniture, good lighting – and an elegant collection of simple carved heads from all over the world. Bedrooms are crisp, bathrooms modern with luxurious accessories; wallow and gaze down to the sea. Birdlife abounds, soft fruits are served, Rye is a very short drive.

The garden

The house is an attractive mix of old and new; so too is the garden. Linda and Stuart inherited some lovely old trees, a wood once frequented by smugglers, a pond and a happy wisteria, then added their own personality. The garden is in different sections: formal at the front, terraced and bowl-shaped at the back, with fabulous views to the sea. A parterre provides cut flowers and some fruit and vegetables; Linda has a love of grasses, shaped beds and striking plants, many in dark reds, oranges and whites. Everything curves here – gateways and steps – to match the bowl shape. For height there are vertical railway sleepers, and a minimalist courtyard with a reflection pool, steel girders and climbers. At the front, a formal garden is developing. Wildlife is abundant: kestrels lurk in the bowl, badgers bumble at night (and eat the Harlands' figs, mischievous things). The terrace around the house has good seating areas and there is a glass-covered veranda so you can admire the views all year round. Great Dixter, Sissinghurst and Pashley Manor are close, should you need further inspiration. *NGS, RHS.*

Details

- Rooms: 2 doubles.
- Price: £110-£140.
- Meals: Pub 600 yards. Restaurants in Rye, 3 miles.
- Ethical Collection: Community. See page 10.

On your doorstep
- Bateman's: Kipling's formal English Arts & Crafts garden, free entry in Nov/Dec
- Smallhythe Place: former home of the Victorian actress Ellen Terry, with rose garden, orchard & nuttery

Top tip
Let plants seed themselves: they'll develop healthily where they settle

Contact

Linda & Stuart Harland
Knellstone House,
Udimore, Rye TN31 6AR

01797 222410
07818 402450 (mobile)
info@knellstonehouse.co.uk
www.knellstonehouse.co.uk

Map: see page 96

Boarsney

Three acres of topiary, garden rooms, kitchen garden & a lake you can row

The house

You are met by smiley Lois and her three lovely dogs. Walk straight in to the main front hall with its squashy sofas and a wood-burning stove – perfect for roosting with a book on a chilly day. Quiet bedrooms have sloping ceilings, are criss-crossed with ancient beams and painted in soft colours; beds are worth sinking into and bathrooms are immaculate. Wake to soft fruits from the garden, hot smoked salmon, bread from the local bakers, full English; timings are flexible and you can eat on the terrace with the birds on sunny days. No standing on ceremony here, all is serene.

The garden

A delightful three-acre garden with a lake, two islands, a jetty housing geese and ducks, and a large fish-filled pond patrolled by a gloomy heron. Lois inherited this just two years ago but it all looks effortlessly mature and as much as possible is grown from seed. Outside the house is a large south-facing terrace overlooking smooth lawns and flower-filled borders. A formal garden with hedging, paths and topiary leads down to the walled kitchen garden, its mellow walls matching those of the house; here Lois grows her organic vegetables, peaches, flowers and soft fruits for the table. Further beds are filled with her favourite old roses for delicious scents, alongside old-fashioned perennials planted in swathes of colour. Established trees include contorted willows, *Cercis canadensis* 'Forest Pansy' and a monkey puzzle; throughout are benches and hidden places – lovely spots for watching very fat birds, or just to unwind. Wander through the knot garden from which there are heavenly views across farmland. Take a rowing boat on the lake, sizzle by the outdoor pool on sunny days. Lois calls herself a novice but she has done a magnificent job so far, and has oodles of plans for the future.

Details

- Rooms: 2 doubles.
- Price: £90. Singles £60.
- Meals: Pubs/restaurants 0.5 miles.

On your doorstep
- Sissinghurst Castle: the most famous 20th-century garden in England; based on garden rooms, including the exquisite White Garden
- Bedgebury Pinetum: collection of conifers open all year

Top tip
Learn to sow seeds: it saves a fortune in a large garden

Contact

Lois Denning
Boarsney,
Boadiam Road,
Saleshurst,
Robertsbridge TN32 5SR

01580 860334
loisdenning@btconnect.com

Map: see page 96

Lamberden Cottage

Lovely informal garden with differing borders, corners & wildlife

The house

Down a farm track find two 1780 cottages knocked into one, with flagstone floors, a cheery wood-burner in the guest sitting room and welcoming Beverley and Branton. There's a traditional country cottage feel with pale walls, thick oak beams, soft carpeting and very comfortable bedrooms (the twin has a child's bedroom adjoining); views from all are across the Weald of Kent. Trip down to the lovely gardens to find your own private spot, sip a sundowner on the terrace, eat well in the restful family dining room. Near to Sissinghurst, Great Dixter and many historic places.

The garden

Lily of the valley perfumes the air, Millie and Millicent (the statues) peek out, ducks waddle happily and the secret garden beckons. Here is a truly English garden whirling with Beverley's old favourites: crocosmia, epimedium, euphorbias and day lilies. Wander the walled garden with its pretty borders; swathes of soft and a sprinkling of hot colours explode across the two neat acres; a border bursts with hellebores, another spills over with apricot, dark blue and night-blue bearded irises. Snoozy seating areas are dotted around, one has a grape vine clambering the wall, the other is shaded beneath a tumbling rose arbour; trees swish and sway in the paddock – copper beech, walnut, elder, a group of silver birch: all have been planted for family and friends in the many years the Screetons have lived here; the latest edition is a mulberry tree for their youngest grandson. Six fruit trees – two plum, two apple, a pear and a damson – along with veg from the raised brick beds are for guests to enjoy and if you're lucky you may spot a family of greater-spotted woodpeckers; the bird tables, nut-holders and nesting boxes make a happy home for all sorts. The family get infinite pleasure from their garden and ask only that you do too.

Details		Contact
• Rooms: 2 doubles, 1 twin.	**On your doorstep**	Beverley & Branton Screeton
• Price: From £70. Singles from £55.	• Great Dixter: long grasses spangled with flowers & wonderful colour combinations	Lamberden Cottage, Rye Road, Sandhurst, Cranbrook TN18 5PH
• Meals: Dinner £22.	• Marle Place: walled scented gardens & orchid collection	01580 850743
		07768 462070 (mobile)
		thewalledgarden@lamberdencottage.co.uk
		www.lamberdencottage.co.uk
	Top tip	
	To beat sawfly, add mulch in autumn & remove with their larvae in spring	Map: see page 96

Hornbeams

Relaxing informal garden dominated by sweeping Kentish views

The house

Rolling hills and woodland, long views over luscious Kent, and a lovely garden that Alison has created entirely herself. This is a modern bungalow, a rare phenomenon in this book, a Scandia house brick-built from a Swedish kit. It is brilliant for wheelchair users and altogether easy and comfortable to be in, with floral-covered sofas and chairs and plain reproduction furniture. Alison, a beauty therapist and masseuse, is friendly and gracious. The house is so close to Dover that it is worth staying here for the night before embarking on the ferry fray.

The garden

Perfectly designed, brilliantly executed – Alison has come a long way since this garden was a field. She used to picnic here as a child, admire the view and dream about living here... Now the garden surrounds the house and is bursting with plants. At the front are roses, camellias, lavender and acers in pots; a blackthorn and hawthorn hedge is grown through with golden hop, vines and more roses. By the front gate is a spring bed, then a purple bed leading to a white-scented border of winter flowering clematis and magnolias. An immaculate herb garden is spiked with tall fennel, the vegetable garden has raised beds and a morello cherry tree, and the orchard hums with fecundity. Winter and autumn beds are filled with interest and colour: snake-bark maple, dusky pink chrysanthemums, witch hazel and red-stemmed cornus. The herbaceous border is a triumph – colours move from pinks, purples and blues through apricots, creams and whites to the 'hot' end, and self-seeded intruders are swiftly dealt with. A little waterfall surrounded by lilies sits in the pond garden and rockery where hostas, ferns, astilbes, gunnera, bamboo and lilac compete for space. Rejoice in the knowledge that someone who has achieved their dream is so happy to share it with others. *RHS, Barham Horticultural Society.*

Details

- Rooms: 1 double, 1 twin, 1 single.
- Price: £75-£85. Singles £50.
- Meals: Occasional dinner £20. Pubs 1 mile.
- Travel Club offer: 10% off stays of 2 or more nights.

On your doorstep
- Goodnestone Park Gardens: come for Feb's snowdrop Sundays, spring blossom in the arboretum, foxgloves in the woodland garden
- Local woodland: at its finest with swathes of bluebells in April/May

Top tip
Don't fight against the odds: only grow plants that like your soil & aspect

Contact

Alison Crawley
Hornbeams, Jesses Hill,
Kingston, Canterbury CT4 6JD

01227 830119
07798 601016 (mobile)
hornbeamsbandb@btinternet.com
www.hornbeams.co.uk

Map: see page 96

photographs © Frances Webster

Rock Farm House

A two-acre cottage garden bursting with flowers all through the year

The house

This is a charming Kentish farmhouse, its beams fashioned from recycled ships' timbers from Chatham dockyard. Bedrooms are simple, traditional, lovely, one with a four-poster bed. Walls are pale or pure white, bedheads floral and furniture antique; the bedroom in the Victorian extension has a barrel ceiling and two big windows that look eastwards over the bog garden to the glorious Kentish Weald. Stairs lead down into the dining room with its lovely old log fire. Expect free-range eggs from the farm, homemade jams and local honey for breakfast.

The garden

Plantsmen will be happy here. In the seventies, when her children were young, Sue ran a nursery at Rock Farm that built up a considerable reputation. It closed in 2000, but her collection of interesting plants continues to be celebrated in her own garden. She knows from experience what plants grow best in these alkaline conditions, and they perform for her. The evergreen *Berberis stenophylla* provides a striking backdrop to the large herbaceous border – 90-foot long and, in places, 35-foot wide. Bulbs grown along the hedge are superceded by herbaceous plants; as these grow, the dying bulb foliage behind is neatly hidden from view. The oriental poppies in May herald the outburst of colour that lasts from June to September, and, to encourage wildlife, cutting down is delayed until January. The bog garden that lies below the house is filled with candelabra primulas, trollius, astilbes, day lilies, gunnera, lythrum, filipendulas and arum lilies: a continuous flowering from April to July. In a further area – around two natural ponds – contrasting conifer foliage interplanted with herbaceous perennials is set against a backdrop of Kentish woodland; superb groupings of hostas and ferns grow in shady areas. A delightful spot. *NGS, Good Gardens Guide, RHS Garden Finder.*

Details		Contact
• Rooms: 1 double, 2 twins. • Price: £75. Singles £50. • Meals: Restaurant within 1 mile.	**On your doorstep** • Ightham Mote: hidden valley garden of 14th-century manor: long cottage borders, vegetables interplanted with herbs, wilder areas of rhododendrons & Grade I-listed dog kennel **Top tip** A good mulch feeds plants & stops weeds	Sue Corfe Rock Farm House, Gibbs Hill, Nettlestead, Maidstone ME18 5HT 01622 812244 www.rockfarmhousebandb.co.uk Map: see page 96

Wickham Lodge

A riverside garden of peace, tranquillity & wonderful surprises

The house

The one-time gatehouse to the big house on the hill looks Georgian, but started life Tudor: two lodges woven into one. Cherith spoils you with traditional comforts; you'll love the riverside setting and the log-warmed drawing room with the greenest view. The bedroom overlooking the river is fresh and airy with linen quilts on white metal beds; the Tudor Room is low-ceilinged with pretty pine and Victorian-style 'rain bath' (amazing). Have breakfast in the garden, lunch in Canterbury and supper in the village; its pubs, restaurants and 14th-century bridge ooze history and charm.

The garden

Who would believe so much fecundity could be squeezed into one half acre? Cherith has known and loved this walled garden – 14 small gardens that flow into one – for over 40 years. Many plants were used in Tudor times (the business of identification is unfaltering), with cottage garden plants being popped in over the years. Starting at the top end is the kitchen garden, a horn of plenty cultivated wisely, 'companion planting' controlling pests and diseases. Then a fruit grove, a secret garden, a Cornish haven, a rose walk fragrant with over one hundred Old English shrub roses. In the Japanese garden, a stairway of railway sleepers topped with pebbles winds serenely up to a circular terrace enfolded by winter flowering shrubs. Later this transforms into a cool green oasis, while the most central section of the garden opens up to its summery palette of purples, pinks, whites and blues. Wander further... to the gravelled hop garden, where a rustic pergola supports hops from the river bank, and a topiary terrace (with goldfish pond) nudges the Tudor back of the house. To the front, a boatyard garden by the river – boats bob by at high tide, birds at low. The drive is edged with lavender and you park among vines.

Details

- Rooms: 1 double, 1 twin/double, 1 single.
- Price: £90. Singles £45-£55.
- Meals: Pubs/restaurants 100 yards.
- Use your Sawday's Gift Card here.
- Ethical Collection: Food. See page 10.

On your doorstep
- Museum of Kent Life: 62 varieties of apple trees & 149 different types of herbs
- Wylesford Village: trees displaying beautiful autumn colours line the riverbank

Top tip
A garden is a living space: work with it & it will be happy

Contact

Richard & Cherith Bourne
Wickham Lodge,
The Quay, 73 High Street,
Aylesford ME20 7AY

01622 717267
wickhamlodge@aol.com
www.wickhamlodge.co.uk

Map: see page 96

24 Fox Hill

Town garden – gradually being re-landscaped by vigorous resident chickens

The house

This part of London is full of sky, trees and wildlife; Pissarro captured on canvas the view up the hill in 1870 (the painting is in the National Gallery). There's good stuff everywhere – things hang off walls and peep over the tops of dressers; bedrooms are stunning, with antiques, textiles, paintings and big, firm beds. Sue, a graduate from Chelsea Art College, employs humour and intelligence to put guests at ease and has created a special garden, too. Tim often does breakfasts. Frogs sing at night, woodpeckers wake you in the morning, in this lofty, peaceful retreat.

The garden

The Haighs' home in the sweet seclusion of Fox Hill has a small gravelled front garden with bobbles of box and a standard bay – an eye-catching frontage for the pretty Victorian house – but there's much, much more to come. The long rectangular back garden has been completely re-designed and now bursts with colour and interest in every direction. Sue, who once worked at the Chelsea Physic Garden and is a true plant-lover, has cleared and re-planted paved areas by the house and built a raised pond for her beloved fish. The delicate water plants are guarded by feathery grasses that thrust skywards from their containers. Climbers snake up walls, trellises and an arch, while water cascades soothingly from a waterfall into the pond. She has nurtured a few of the plants that were there when she arrived, a thriving ceanothus and a weeping pear tree among them, but otherwise started with a clean slate. To add a final flourish and to mark her pleasure at having her first-ever garden shed to play with, she has planted a slender crab apple outside its door. This is a garden packed with promise. *RHS, RSPB.*

Photographs © Rob Cousins

Details		Contact

- Rooms: 1 double, 1 twin/double, 1 twin.
- Price: £90-£120. Singles £50.
- Meals: Dinner £35. Pubs/restaurants 5-minute walk.
- Travel Club offer: Jar of house preserve in room. Pick-up from local station. Bottle of house wine with dinner.

On your doorstep
- Crystal Palace Park: hunt for dinosaurs in this Victorian pleasure ground & explore the Tea Maze
- Horniman Museum & Gardens: a lively & varied oasis with superb city views

Top tip
Grow salads & herbs in raised beds to keep them away from chickens!

Sue & Tim Haigh
24 Fox Hill,
Crystal Palace,
London SE19 2XE

020 8768 0059
suehaigh@hotmail.co.uk
www.foxhill-bandb.co.uk

Map: see page 96

Essex

Mount Hall

Wide lawns & fine trees framed by formal herbaceous borders

The house

A beautiful listed Queen Anne house. The upstairs rooms are large, light, quietly faded and comfortable, with garden flowers and garden views; for those who prefer independence – and for wheelchairs – the garden room is an excellent size, with a huge sofa, maps and guide books aplenty and its own front door. Bathrooms are old-fashioned but spotless, and Eleanor, young, charming and friendly, gives you delicious homemade preserves at breakfast. Set out from this peaceful place to explore Constable country, and the beautiful villages of Nayland, Stoke-by-Nayland and Dedham.

The garden

The drive sweeps you around and up to the handsome pillared and stuccoed front porch of Mount Hall, overlooking a wide lawn flanked by mature trees and shrubs. The family have a great interest in trees and the many well-established varieties act as a dramatic backdrop to the labour-saving foliage plants which speak for themselves through their different shapes and shades of green and yellow. This is a place for retreat, very tranquil, with plenty of seats under trees, or by the pool. The walled pool garden is totally secluded and private, a haven of peace watched over by a huge eucalyptus; planting is cool, calm and subdued. A beautiful evergreen tapestry border is of year-round interest in muted greens; elsewhere greys and whites, pale blues and silver predominate, most of the plants coming from the Beth Chatto Gardens eight miles away. The pool was an erstwhile swimming pool: the formal rectangular shape has been kept, but now teems with wildlife. Nicknamed the "gosh" pool after visitors' first reactions, the fish and frogs have bred and multiplied well since its conversion. So peaceful, four miles from the edge of the Dedham Vale, and close to the oldest recorded town of Colchester. *HPS*.

Details

- Rooms: 1 double, 2 twins/doubles.
- Price: £80. Singles from £50.
- Meals: Pub 1 mile.
- Travel Club offer: 10% off room rate Monday to Thursday.

On your doorstep
- Beth Chatto Gardens: accomplished contrasts, from lush perennials to the evergreens & greys of the arid drought garden
- Flatford Mill: setting of Constable's 'The Hay Wain,' & a riverside walk to Bridge Cottage (NT) for tea

Top tip
Plant garlic under peach trees to prevent leaf curl

Contact

Eleanor Carbutt
Mount Hall,
Great Horkesley, Colchester CO6 4BZ

01206 271359
07767 608437 (mobile)
emcarbutt@gmail.com
www.mounthall.co.uk

Map: see page 96

Abbey House

Majestic trees & showy shrubs
in a peaceful three acres

The house

A spectacular arrival. Find a handsome, listed, Dutch-gabled house (1846) fronted by an impressive fishpond upon which black swans glide. On land, the peacocks lord it over the chickens. Sue's welcome is warm and easy, her bedrooms simply and comfortably arranged, each with a couple of armchairs and garden or pond views. High ceilings and large windows make for a light, tranquil atmosphere. Settle down in front of the fire in the guest drawing room, or wander out through French windows to the shrub walk. Breakfast sausages and bacon are local; the eggs are from just outside.

The garden

Fine old trees – oaks, limes, beeches and weeping willows – dignify the three acres of garden and seven of meadowland surrounding Sue's Victorian rectory on the site of an ancient abbey; evidence of her love of gardening – and her talent for it – is all around you. Early flowering yellow banksia climbs the front of the house, fighting for the limelight with the *Clematis montana* that tumbles around the door. The heated pool (which you may use if you ask) lies enclosed in a sheltered suntrap surrounded by trellises of fragrant honeysuckle, jasmine and trachelospermum. Several passion flowers run riot and there's a gravel bed for hot- and dry-lovers:

Japanese banana, agapanthus, verdant bamboo and interesting ornamental grasses. Plenty of new shrubs have gone in this year and the shrub walk also parades many mature plants including viburnum and rubus 'Benenden'. This is a thoroughly peaceful space to amble around: sit and contemplate a game of croquet under the magnificent copper beech, admire the swans and ducks in the lovely pond lined with flag irises – best viewed from a picturesque arched wooden bridge. Then wander at will in the woodland with its early carpet of snowdrops and aconites; further afield you will find a small flock of sheep and assorted fowl. *Village 'open garden.'*

Details		Contact
• Rooms: 2 doubles, 1 twin. • Price: £70–£90. Singles £35–£45. • Meals: Pubs 2.5 miles.	**On your doorstep** • Helmingham Hall: imposing moated garden of unique parts cleverly linked by flowing bridges & tunnels • Fox Fritillary Meadow, Framsden: six glorious acres of snake's head fritillaries, best in April/May **Top tip** Plant fragrant shrubs by garden gates & catch a waft of scent on passing	Sue Bagnall Abbey House, Monk Soham, Framlingham IP13 7EN 01728 685225 sue@abbey-house.net www.abbey-house.net Map: see page 96

Bressingham Hall

Celebrated informal gardens
- an inspiration for gardeners
& designers

The house

Past the famous steam museum and on to the house, built in 1780 for the Squire of Bressingham. It's a handsome place with high ceilings, large sash windows and sensational garden views. The interiors are deeply old-fashioned and that is part of the charm. You breakfast in a sunny, east-facing room on Grandad's rhubarb baked with brown sugar, locally cured bacon and farm eggs. Discover a sitting room with an open log fire and views, big bedrooms filled with books, magazines and easy chairs, and good clean bathrooms. Your host Ian is delightful. *Min. two nights at weekends.*

The garden

In 1953 Alan Bloom, founder of the legendary nursery and Dell Garden, wanted to experiment with new ways of growing hardy perennials in island beds. He first planted in front of the family home and as soon as he realised they were successful he planted in nearby meadows, eventually accumulating 48 beds covering six acres. By 1962 he had collected 5,000 species and varieties. His son Adrian joined the business in 1962 and became keen to do his own thing, initially using mainly conifers and heathers in Foggy Bottom Garden. Over the years Foggy Bottom has developed as a spectacular garden of year-round interest. The whole family have a passion for plants and the growth continues in the Summer Garden; it holds the National Collection of miscanthus. Adrian's Wood is bulging with North American origin plants, the Winter Garden is spectacular with its colourful cornus, snowdrops, early bulbs and hellebores, and the Fragrant Garden is packed with scented plants. It is a privilege to stay here, in the midst of these world-renowned gardens – and, of course, you can buy plants and take them home. Whether you have a large plot, a tiny patch or just pots to fill there is inspiration for all.

Photographs © Richard and Adrian Bloom

Details

- Rooms: 1 double, 1 twin, 1 family room.
- Price: £85. Singles £55.
- Meals: Pub/restaurant 400 yards.

On your doorstep
- Bressingham Steam Museum, next door (free entry for guests): puff through the gardens & woodland on a steam train
- Lopham Fen: a delightful walk in reinstated fen: spot the Polish Konik ponies

Top tip
To deter deer, hang a piece of soap above the plants they like

Contact

Ian Tilden
Bressingham Hall,
Bressingham,
Diss IP22 2AA

01379 687243
b&b@bressinghamgardens.com
www.bressinghamgardens.com

Map: see page 96

Norfolk

Sallowfield Cottage

A deceptive one acre, with crammed cottage borders & a big glassy pond

The house

In a beautifully remote part of Norfolk is a hospitable house crammed with treasures: prints and paintings, polished family pieces, leather fender seats by the drawing room fire. One bedroom, not huge but handsome, has a canopied bed and decoration to suit the house (1850); another room is on the ground floor. Drift into the garden to find a jungly pond with a jetty on which you breakfast (deliciously): magical in spring and summer. Caroline gives you the best, her lovely lurchers add to the charm, and if you have friends locally she can do lunch for up to ten. *Over nines welcome.*

The garden

A deceptive one acre, but the beautiful large pond in front of the house acts as a huge mirror and reflects tall trees, island beds and the building itself, giving a Norwegian 'lake impression' of space and green. When Caroline arrived it was swamped and overgrown; she only left what she decided was interesting. This included an impressive swamp cypress, a weeping ash, lots of viburnums, magnolias, a chimonanthus and an as yet unidentified acer she calls the "firework tree" because of its fiery autumn colour. There are also some very old trees: an enormous willow and a vast ash. Caroline has a real knack for positioning plants – they all thrive where they're placed and look good together; lilacs and pinks, shades of green and the odd splash of dark red or yellow against the perfect backdrop. An old ditch has been turned into a sunken path with a trimmed hedge on one side and a herbaceous bank on the other. Clematis and honeysuckle wind through trees and shrubs and all the shapes and colours are soft – there's no ugly rigidity. A tiny, enclosed courtyard has been constructed against one wall of the house and a pink *Clematis texensis* shoots up it; another wall is capped by curly tiles and there are pots filled with hostas. The pale terracotta-floored conservatory is prettily canopied with vine leaves. *NGS.*

Details

- Rooms: 2 doubles, 1 twin.
- Price: £65. Singles £40.
- Meals: Lunch £15. Dinner from £25. Pub 2.5 miles.

On your doorstep
- East Ruston Old Vicarage: a 'must' – with two magnolias at their finest in April
- Lower Wood, Ashwellthorpe: rare ancient woodland, delightful bluebells & wood anemones in spring

Top tip
Check clematis stems at ground level for slug damage

Contact

Caroline Musker
Sallowfield Cottage, Wattlefield,
Wymondham, Norwich NR18 9NX

01953 605086
07778 316616 (mobile)
caroline.musker@tesco.net
www.sallowfieldcottage.co.uk

Map: see page 96

Norfolk

Litcham Hall

A much-loved family garden still evolving after forty years

The house

This was Litcham's doctor's house and today, over 200 years after it was built, the red-brick Hall remains at the centre of the community. This is a thoroughly English home with elegant proportions; the hall, drawing room and dining room are gracious and beautifully furnished. The big-windowed guest rooms look onto the stunning garden where you are free to wander. Household hens lay breakfast's eggs, and the garden gives soft fruit for the table in season. John and Hermione are friendly and charming; you're half an hour from the coast. *Children, dogs & use of pool by arrangement.*

The garden

This superb garden has given the family a lot of pleasure over the 40 years since they came to Litcham Hall. The pool has provided fun for children and visitors, but John and Hermione have found the design and planting of their garden from scratch the most satisfying project. Yew hedges make a dramatic backdrop for herbaceous borders and the framework for a sunken area with a little lily pond and fountain. Strolling along mown paths through their wild garden is a delight in spring when the snowdrops, azaleas and bluebells are out: in summer you emerge from this spinney through a pergola covered in climbing roses. Behind the house the pool is sheltered in part of a double-walled garden, with a brick-arched veranda loggia down one side – a wonderful spot, especially in Mediterranean weather. The walled Italian garden was inspired by the desire to put to best use some beautiful inherited stone urns. Now artfully positioned in a parterre of lavender-filled, box-edged beds, the urns make an elegant finishing touch to a formal composition entirely suited to the period of the house.

Details

- Rooms: 2 doubles, 1 twin.
- Price: £70-£90.
  Singles by arrangment.
- Meals: Pub/restaurant 3 miles.
- Travel Club offer: 10% off room rate Mon-Thurs. 10% off stays of 2 or more nights.

On your doorstep
- Sandringham: the finest of all Royal gardens promises 60 acres of year-round interest
- Castle Acre Priory: beautifully preserved home to a recreated monastic herb garden

Top tip
Prune fruit-bearing stems of redcurrant efficiently & then gather the fruit

Contact

John & Hermione Birkbeck
Litcham Hall,
Litcham,
King's Lynn PE32 2QQ

01328 701389
hermionebirkbeck@hotmail.com
www.litchamhall.co.uk

Map: see page 96

Spindrift

A secret paradise of borders, walkways & fountains

The house

A long, architect-designed 1933 house in a charming, sleepy village, home of the Quaker Movement; timbers from the Mayflower came to rest in an old barn nearby. Much of the house is open to guests and Norma is an accomplished cook; fruits, herbs and vegetables appear on the table, flowers are beautifully arranged. Traditional bedrooms are super comfortable with excellent beds, powerful new showers, and pretty floral curtains. Swim in the heated pool, walk the stunning countryside, or just slump in the sitting room with its French windows open to the scented garden.

The garden

Norma – "chlorophyll gives me a kick!" – has loved plants since her grandmother took her to Kew when she was very young. As soon as she realised that the garden at Spindrift was a similar shape to Monet's, off she went into arches, walkways, a heavenly series of 'rooms', beautiful herbaceous borders and fountains, all floodlit at night. It is all on different levels. There's a violet-strewn dell with newts, toads and frogs in the pond, fine lawns to the front flanked by colourful borders and, to one side, a heated, kidney-shaped pool in a sunny raised area with lots of pretty pots (packed with tulips in spring). The fruit and vegetable gardens are terraced down a hill and produce 29 different varieties of vegetable and 13 of fruit, all for the table. There is a large garden room where meals can be served in fine weather, a circular theme for the arched doorways and walkways, and a pristine hosta corner showing off different varieties (not a sign of lace: snails and slugs are somehow deterred) surrounding a raised fountain. Norma is very 'hands on' and often takes children from the school next door around the garden for nature and art. Colours are muted, the softest pinks, blues and mauves backed up by every conceivable green, silver and grey from her beloved hostas.

Details		Contact

Details

- Rooms: 1 double, 1 twin.
- Price: £130. Singles £75.
- Meals: Lunch £25. Dinner, 4 courses with wine, £30. Packed lunch £12.50. Pub 2 miles.
- Travel Club offer: 10% off room rate Mon-Thurs. Free pick-up from local train station.
- Ethical Collection: Community; Food. See page 10.

On your doorstep
- Hughenden Manor: Disraeli's retreat, lately restored to his wife's 1860s design, embracing Victorian lawns & terraces, an apple & pear orchard stocked with traditional varieties & a walled garden

Top tip
Constant vigilance: keep it neat with nowhere for slugs & bugs to hide

Contact

Norma Desmond-Mawby
Spindrift,
Jordans HP9 2TE

01494 873172
07963 661788 (mobile)
johnmawby@hotmail.com
www.spindrift.biz

Map: see page 96

Town Farm Cottage

Secrets, sounds & scents –
you must walk round more
than once!

The house

A dream setting – and a picture-perfect farmhouse,
built along traditional lines beside the lakes and on
the edge of acres of farmland. The guest drawing
room is large and light with a door to the garden for
sunny evenings. Bedrooms have garden views,
Victorian brass beds, pretty cushions and fresh
flowers; even a little decanter of sherry and a fridge
outside for your own wine. Wake up to the smell of
freshly baked bread – part of Jim's hearty
breakfasts. Independence lovers will prefer the new
garden lodge with its own little kitchen and
veranda. *Minimum two nights.*

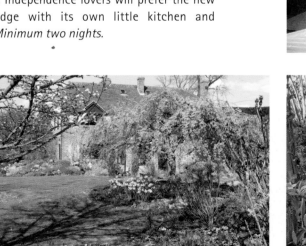

The garden

Theresa started taking gardening seriously years ago, when she and Jim moved into their home on their Oxfordshire farm. It all began with a rockery and is now a maturing multi-dimensional plant paradise. What was once sheep pasture is now one-and-a-half acres of superbly planted, well-designed areas that range from the formal to the wonderfully wild. Theresa has created rockeries, scree beds and dramatic borders as well as a restful waterfall and a lake. The garden is divided into a series of well-defined areas, each with a mood of its own and with witty decorations including an old telephone kiosk and street lamp. You'll find a rose-smothered pergola, an ornamental grass border, specimen trees, and gloriously manicured lawns. Theresa is a self-confessed plantaholic and avidly collects new treasures – no wonder the garden has been featured in the *Sunday Telegraph* and on *Gardener's World*! 'Albertine' roses wind through apple trees, a vigorous 'American Pillar' decorates an arch. Best of all is the lake, with its walk and fringes of water iris, mature shrubs and water-loving plants; home to ducks and moorhen. Visiting geese and kites, together with a host of native birds, are a pleasure to watch from the lawn or a scented, tucked away corner of the garden. A gem. *RHS*.

Details		Contact
• Rooms: 2 doubles, 1 single. Self-catered lodge for 2.	**On your doorstep**	Theresa & Jim Clark Town Farm Cottage, Brook Street, Kingston Blount OX39 4RZ
• Price: £75-£100. Singles £60.	• The Chilterns: lambing in April & bluebell woods in May	
• Meals: Pubs/restaurants 600 yards.	• Waterperry Gardens: acres of colour begin yearly with the	01844 352152
• Travel Club offer: 20% off stays of 3 or more nights.	sequenced spring bulbs; a joyous variety of plants & growing	07971 436504 (mobile) theresa@townfarmcottage.co.uk
• Ethical Collection: Food. See page 10.	methods on show	www.townfarmcottage.co.uk
	Top tip Buy your wisteria in bloom so you can be sure it will flower	Map: see page 96

Blackwell Grange

A combination of Cotswold country charm & old-fashioned scents

The house

Thatch barns and stables dated 1604, and wonderfully creative touches at a Cotswold farmhouse revived by a talented third generation. Didi, interior designer, has introduced patterned silks and restored antiques to creaking floorboards and flagstones; elegant bedrooms have dressing gowns, fine linen, indulgent treats. You breakfast on home-produced eggs and sausages, and fruits from the grandparents' orchard. Pictures of the family's racehorses dot the sitting room, while views from mullioned windows reach over the gardens to pedigree livestock. Ideal for theatre lovers and walkers.

The garden

A former rickyard for the farm has been worked into a pretty English garden around the farmhouse. Old York stones with curved raised beds form grand steps up to the lawn; apple trees pop up through hedges; honeysuckle, clematis and jasmine climb through them. There's a relaxed feel to all the planting and no strict colour schemes which the third generation and their young family want to maintain, but plans are afoot to develop more design-led areas without disturbing the fluent and charming rhythm that flows from the garden to the countryside. Perfectly clipped hedges, neat lawns and careful planting around arches and pergolas show a more restrained side to the garden but somehow it all looks effortless anyway. Ancient barns have been used as scaffolding for the old roses and hops which give colour on different levels, and there are plenty of quiet spots to sit and enjoy it. A circular stone seat hides behind a wall at the end of the barns where Didi and William are gradually adding roses, transferring plants from their garden in Cornwall and creating a cut flower bed. Bantams and ducks roam here; lamb, pigs and cattle are reared too: always available for your freezer. This is a garden to come back and visit time and again.

Details

- Rooms: 1 double, 1 twin/double.
- Price: £85-£95. Singles from £60.
- Meals: Pubs 1-1.5 miles.
- Travel Club offer: Local and homemade food/produce in your room.

On your doorstep
- Armscote Manor: high spots are the fiery red borders & the serene silver garden; one of several nearby open for NGS
- Hidcote: often mentioned in summer, but as exceptional in spring

Top tip
Copper tape under the rim of a hosta pot & pebbles on the soil guarantee no slugs

Contact

William & Didi Vernon Miller
Blackwell Grange,
Blackwell,
Shipston-on-Stour CV36 4PF

01608 682357
didi@blackwellgrange.co.uk
www.blackwellgrange.co.uk

Map: see page 96

The Old Manor House

Series of small garden rooms, spilling over with loveliness & roses

The house

There is a timelessness about this elegant, very old village house, which Jane runs with energy and friendliness. A pretty blue twin bedroom and a single room are in the wing with its own large, elegant drawing and dining room – it's seductively easy to relax and perfect for families or friends. The A-shaped double, with ancient beams and oak furniture, is in the main part of the house, with a lovely bathroom and sharing the drawing and dining rooms. Wander down the garden to the gentle Stour, join a special walk from the village or hole up at the pub. Lovely.

The garden

All garden lovers, but rosarians in particular, will adore the garden Jane and William have created over the years. With a background of high mature trees and a sloping site, they have built a series of loosely, rather than formally, linked areas, adding beech and yew hedges vigorously and sympathetically to make a garden that sits well with their lovely old home. Old roses rule above all, climbing up walls, rambling over pergolas and arches, softening hard corners and, in a final flourish, scenting and colouring a rose avenue. There is a blend of the stiffer hybrid teas, which Jane inherited and can't find the heart to remove, and a riot of treasures from sources including Peter Beales.

Jane is sending vigorous climbers like 'Kiftsgate' rocketing up the trees in the orchard – a gorgeous sight – but there is much, much more: cleverly planted borders, a delicious herb garden where sage, fennel, thyme and others rub shoulders, delightful colour-theming in flower beds bursting with good plants and so many details as well as a glorious overall feel to enjoy. William has strong ideas about design, Jane has strong ideas about plants and planting. Between them, they have made the very best of the lay of their three acres and their love of plants and garden design is infectious.

Details		Contact
• Rooms: 1 double. Wing: 1 twin, 1 single. • Price: From £85. Singles from £50. • Meals: Restaurants nearby.	**On your doorstep** • Kiftsgate: generations of women gardeners have nurtured the snowy 50ft-high rambler, 'Kiftsgate Rose' • Upton House: the National Collection of Asters, in full bloom in Sept **Top tip** For a drift of daffodils, fling a handful of bulbs over grass & plant them where they fall & roll	Jane Pusey The Old Manor House, Halford, Shipston-on-Stour CV36 5BT 01789 740264 07786 467916 (mobile) info@oldmanor-halford.fsnet.co.uk www.oldmanor-halford.co.uk Map: see page 96

Salford Farm House

Delicious borders, and old roses & clematis on weathered oak support

The house

Beautiful within, handsome without. Subtle colours, oak beams and lovely old pieces: Jane has achieved a seductive combination of comfort and style. A flagstoned hallway and an old rocking horse, ticking clocks, beeswax and fresh flowers speak of a much-loved house. Jane was a ballet teacher, Richard has green fingers. Dinners are superb: meat and game from the Ragley Estate, delicious fruits in season. Bedrooms have a soft, warm elegance and flat-screen TVs, bathrooms are spotless and welcoming, views are to garden or fields. Wholly delightful – worth a serious detour.

The garden

An enchanting garden that flows from one space to another, studded with rare and interesting plants. It is also divided by a wing of the house, so you pass under an open-sided brick and timber barn (a wonderful seated area for lazy summer days) to cross from one side to the other. The garden has matured well thanks to a packed planting of roses, shrubs and herbaceous perennials: Jane has an artist's eye. Beautiful arrangements of plants in pots and a square, formal pond reveal her talent. Clever curvy lawns, as smooth as bowling greens, dotted with island beds, give the illusion of space. There is always another corner to peek around and plenty of height:

a pretty gazebo covered in wisteria, weathered deer-fencing screens, a large pergola the length of one wall. There are natural old log sculptures for fun and urns of floaty pink geum; leggy metal seedpods add a contemporary touch. A garden for all seasons, with tulips in spring (heaps of them), peonies, pinks and penstemon in summer, chrysanthemums and asters in autumn. Richard is MD of Hillers, a mile down the road – an award-winning fruit farm, café, shop and display garden from which you can buy all the inspiration you need to take home. *RHS, occasional open garden.*

Details		Contact

- Rooms: 2 twins/doubles.
- Price: £90. Singles £55.
- Meals: Dinner £25. Restaurant 2.5 miles.
- Ethical Collection: Community; Food. See page 10.

On your doorstep
- Hidcote: one of England's finest, dating from 1907; the Pillar Garden is dominated by yews in parallel paths, the Red Borders perform in the hot months, formal hedged rooms are stuffed with peonies, roses, alliums...

Top tip
Use a good cylinder mower & mow as often as possible

Jane & Richard Beach
Salford Farm House,
Salford Priors,
Evesham WR11 8XN

01386 870000
salfordfarmhouse@aol.com
www.salfordfarmhouse.co.uk

Map: see page 96

Dippersmoor Manor

Lovingly tended hillside garden with views to the Black Mountains

The house

Dating in parts back to the 12th century, the red sandstone house is flanked by a magnificent brick and timber long barn. The bedrooms are traditional, airy and spacious with crisp white linen and views to woodland and pasture towards the south, and mountains to the west. Breakfast is in the dining room, where the fireplace was once used for curing bacon, or under the pergola; on warm evenings, dinners of local produce and home-grown vegetables can be enjoyed under the vine in candlelit privacy. Excellent walking from the house, or just a stroll to the village. Very peaceful.

The garden

Weeping pear, rowan and tulip trees dot the main lawn, buzzards float overhead and owls and bats roost in the barn. This big, secluded, hillside garden, with wonderful views to the Black Mountains, was virtually a field when Amanda and Hexie arrived 30 years ago. It was they who planted the avenue of maturing poplars curving up to the house. A flagstone path leads you through a knot garden to the door, overhung by a vine which has been there since the 1920s. Roses, wisteria, quince and hydrangea scramble haphazardly up the walls and everywhere there are things to engage the eye. At the centre of a terraced lawn stands a stone cider press brimming with plants; next door is a box-hedged rose garden. More roses, lavender and sweet peas scent a square, pretty garden in front of the stone summer house, where swallows nest. The old stables provide a good backdrop to a bright border and a pleached lime hedge screens a productive vegetable patch. Old cider orchards and a bluebell wood are fine places to explore, a pergola festooned with vines and clematis provides dappled shade – just the place to sit with a drink.

Details

- Rooms: 2 doubles, 1 twin.
- Price: From £90. Singles from £55.
- Meals: Dinner from £27.50. Supper from £20. Pub in village.

On your doorstep
- Brecon Beacons: undulating national park full of year-round outdoor appeal
- The Weir: a riot of spring bulbs, summer wild flowers & autumn colour along the banks of the Wye

Top tip
Whip climbers into shape with regular pruning & tie back twice a year

Contact

Hexie & Amanda Millais
Dippersmoor Manor,
Kilpeck HR2 9DW

01981 570209
info@dippersmoor.com
www.dippersmoor.com

Map: see page 96

The Old Rectory

Riotous flowers, magnificent trees, croquet & clucking hens: a perfect English garden

The house

A Georgian rectory in the 'golden valley' where Wales and England converge – bliss for walkers. Inside, a comfortable, unpretentious home: family portraits, stuffed birds and Milly the waggy spaniel. Bedrooms are large, airy and filled with good furniture, books, and big windows for garden views; up by the home-grown vegetables find the Black Rock hens who lay breakfast's eggs. There's an elegant drawing room with a grand piano, a dining room with a long table and French windows that open onto the garden. Chrix and Jenny are delightful people and the pub is a stroll.

The garden

Jenny loves her gorgeous garden: three secluded acres at the foot of the Black Mountains. She and Chrix spent months hacking through the undergrowth to uncover lost paths and plants; now the sloping wilderness of long grasses and brambles is unrecognisable. Mature trees – conifers, oak, ash and acacias – provide the backdrop to well-tended lawns and large beds filled to bursting with a variety of plants of many colours. There's a pond, home to newts and frogs, where irises and king cups flourish, a lovingly tended croquet lawn and a summer house that rotates on the upper terrace. The old rectory has some well-pruned roses scrambling up it, and great views of the surrounding countryside from that terrace giving a wonderful feeling of space – in spite of the tall trees. Plenty of evergreens give joy in winter, with roses like 'Kiftsgate' clambering up them, creating quite a display in spring and summer. Huge swathes of lawn are left unmown to protect spring bulbs like daffodils, jonquils and fritillaries. Intentionally leaving some areas untouched has earned the Juckes a wildlife award from the Herefordshire Nature Trust. This garden reflects the character of its owners: relaxed, informal, thoroughly engaging.

Details		Contact
• Rooms: 1 double, 2 twins/doubles. • Price: From £65. Singles from £45. • Meals: Pubs in village.	**On your doorstep** • Abbey Dore Court Gardens: a plant-lovers' garden with captivating herbaceous borders & an arboretum • Kentchurch Court: lovely walled vegetable garden with delicate pergola **Top tip** Support floppy perennials by growing plants through a ball of chicken wire	Jenny Juckes The Old Rectory, Ewyas Harold HR2 0TX 01981 240498 jenny.juckes@btopenworld.com www.theoldrectory.org.uk Map: see page 96

Photographs © Mon Darnbrough

Brobury House

Splendidly restored Victorian riverside gardens with fine views

The house

Here are emerald-green riverbanks, a huge handsome house dominated by a wisteria-cloaked folly and an ancient mulberry on the lawn. Super big bedrooms with traditional wallpapers, polished furniture and carpeted floors have country or garden views – and it's a short dash to the twins' smart shower rooms. After a perfect night's sleep, tuck into locally sourced organic breakfasts on the terrace or in the conservatory – light and lovely, with comfortable seating. Conveniently close to bookish, eccentric Hay-on-Wye, and the 'black and white' village of Weobley.

The garden

Enthusiastic, energetic Pru and Keith are passionate about these gardens that sweep down to the Wye, and have won Green Tourism and Wildlife Action awards for their work. Together with designer Peter Antonius, they are continuing to expand and develop the graceful tree-filled terraces, laid out in the 1880s to make the most of the views. Open to the public (hence the car park at the front and the green signs), this spectacular waterside setting has plenty to explore and places in which to sit and muse. Close to the house the grounds are formal: a south-facing lawn, a lily pond surrounded by acers and a Lutyens-inspired pool with parterre, all overlooking more lawns, and copper beeches, lavender, climbing roses and clipped hornbeam hedges. Rose beds, magnolias, asters and dahlias zing with colour around a pretty pergola and a dramatic Bodmin standing stone. The grounds were once part of a large kitchen garden and vegetables flourish in the original Victorian greenhouses. At the outer reaches, formal gardens give way to the wild, with a natural pond, a mature orchard and a fern garden. The river views take in the church, the ice house and the rectory on the opposite bank where Kilvert lived and is buried. Wildlife thrives on the riverbank: kingfishers are common and you may even spot an otter. *NGS, RHS.*

Details		Contact
• Rooms: 1 double, 1 twin/double, 1 twin. • Price: From £65. Singles from £50. • Meals: Pub 3 miles. • Travel Club offer: One voucher per room to a designated garden within 20 miles of Brobury. Valid for 5 days. Regular change of garden. • Ethical Collection: Environment; Food. See page 10.	**On your doorstep** • Hergest Croft Gardens: nurtured by four generations with stunning Black Mountain views; magnolias in spring, azaleas & giant rhododendrons in summer, blazing maples & birches in autumn **Top tip** To squirrel-proof bulbs in lawns, use a metal stake to make extra deep holes	Pru Cartwright Brobury House, Brobury, Bredwardine HR3 6BS 01981 500229 enquiries@broburyhouse.co.uk www.broburyhouse.co.uk Map: see page 96

Weobley Cross Cottage

English cottage garden with stunning rural views

The house

Come for the wonderful Malvern hills, pasture land dotted with cows and sheep and a pretty Victorian cottage with a neat extension. Inside, tea and biscuits, immaculate bedrooms with floral curtains and old pine, and compact sparkling shower rooms. All is incredibly tickety-boo thanks to Peter's building skills and Anne's talent for co-ordinating colours. You breakfast in the conservatory overlooking the garden on local sausages and organic eggs from their chickens; walk it off in stunning countryside, or head for Malvern with its spring flower show and nearby good nurseries.

The garden

Anne and Peter have clearly poured love, thought and passion into their patch of nearly an acre with stunning views across Herefordshire. In seven years they have transformed an overgrown, concrete-infested wilderness into four delightful areas. Between the house and the forge is the suburban garden with its neatly clipped lawn and flowering shrubs in a wide border; a *Magnolia stellata* in a half barrel is stunning in April and there's a glorious deep red smoke bush. New paths from here take you to a brick-paved, raised patio area, perfect for a drink or breakfast – views are through forsythia, clematis, jasmine and honeysuckle to the pretty cottage garden with its old-fashioned roses, arch rails, grass paths and peaceful pond bustling with dragonflies. In the evening, the lower lawn is the place to be for stunning sunsets among the plum and damson trees; romantics can swing gently in a cushioned seat and watch the clear night sky... you may hear a barn owl too. An abundant kitchen garden area, with greenhouse, also makes a home for the chickens named after grandchildren! Work is divided pretty equally: Peter in charge of vegetables, lawns and hedges, Anne in charge of the plants and borders that she adores to fill with colour and scent. A delightful garden which you are free to explore at your own pace.

Details

- Rooms: 1 double, 1 twin.
- Price: From £65.
- Meals: Pub/restaurant 2 miles.
- Travel Club offer: Pick-up from local train station. Cuttings upon request.

On your doorstep
- Hellens Manor: ancient Hallwood full of anenomes, daffs & bluebells in spring; knot gardens, labyrinth & 1710 avenue of Hellens Early pears
- Berrington Hall: 'Capability' Brown grounds with views

Top tip
For perfect petals, be careful not to wet the flowers when watering geraniums

Contact

Anne & Peter Haywood
Weobley Cross Cottage,
South End Lane, Mathon,
Malvern WR13 5PB

01684 541488
anne@hanleyinteriors.co.uk
www.bedandbreakfastmalvernhills.co.uk

Map: see page 96

Brook Farm

"A fairly chaotic country garden" –
several fecund acres in a valley

The house

A wonderful lost-in-the-country feel here with dogs bounding to greet you, a family of cats lounging around and donkeys looking on. The farmhouse is surprisingly large: you get one end, Sarah and William the other, so there's a private feel. Big armchairs and sofas are made for sprawling, a wood-burner keeps you shiver-free and there are masses of lovely books; you can have a ploughman's supper here if you don't want to budge. Sleep soundly in a charming bedroom with fresh flowers, wake (with tea in bed if you like) to scrambled eggs and delicious smoked trout. A treat.

The garden

Sarah calls this "a nice country garden in a very peaceful valley" but she is too modest. She and William, both keen on natural planting, moved here in 2003 to tackle nine neglected acres; their only rule was that the garden remain in keeping with the land. Around the main house is a cottage garden that froths with blowsy roses, verbascums, alchemilla, peonies, poppies and potentilla; a wisteria-covered pergola is underplanted with tulips and nepeta. To either side are a lavender-edged lawn, and a tidy area of weeping crab apples in gravel quarters with William's alpines underneath; a circular middle bed houses a weeping white rose hugged by chives and alliums. An old tin barn was hauled down to make room for the vegetable garden with its fecund potager: soft fruit, flowers and vegetables rub shoulders happily with forget-me-nots, nigella and foxgloves. Wiggly paths take you to woodland with mature trees, a babbling brook and an old orchard. There's no frantic obsession about weeds and nothing sits uncomfortably in its surroundings – if you have read Mirabel Osler's *A Gentle Plea for Chaos* you will love it here. *NGS*.

Photographs © Julia Stanley

Details

- Rooms: 2 doubles.
- Price: From £80. Singles £65.
- Meals: Supper, ploughman's platter, £35 for 2. Pub/restaurant 2 miles.
- Travel Club offer: Late checkout (12pm). Free pick-up from local bus/train station.
- Ethical Collection: Environment. See page 10.

On your doorstep
- Stockton Bury Gardens: perfect from April to Sept, wheelchair accessible & lovely lunches too
- Burford House: 400 varieties of clematis, Georgian turfed bridge & irresistible garden shop

Top tip
Draw up a proper planting plan before you begin – we didn't!

Contact

Sarah & William Wint
Brook Farm,
Berrington,
Tenbury Wells WR15 8TJ

01584 819868
sarah@brookfarmberrington.com
www.brookfarmberrington.com

Map: see page 96

The Croft Cottage

Wildlife-friendly cottage garden in a five-acre smallholding

The house

Drop from the heights of Clee Hill down narrowing lanes and a secluded valley to find this old estate worker's cottage beside a stream; its new extension is where you will stay: total independence. The Hatchells treat you to eggs from the ducks and hens, homemade marmalade and honey from the bees, as you watch the ducks through the dining room window. Bedrooms are clean, pine-bedded, old-fashioned – not for style fanatics – with comfy chairs; one opens to the garden. Cats and dogs doze, badgers visit, the peace is a balm. *Min. two nights. Dogs welcome to sleep in lobby.*

The garden

The Colly Brook bisects the property, tumbling some 350 yards through the south-facing garden created over ten years by Elizabeth and David – very special. Five bridges now connect the parts of the garden to one another; to the west is a vegetable patch, some herbaceous borders, a willow tunnel and a hazel coppice; to the east are the cottage, more borders, the orchard, the reflective garden and a duck house for the Indian Runner ducks who keep the slugs at bay. Further upstream is the goose field with beehives, geese, chickens and a wildflower meadow which bursts with orchids in June. Beyond this is the wood where there is an observation hide for watching the badgers: a rare treat! A wetland meadow has a pond which is home to moorhens, minnows and dragonflies; hundreds of hedging trees have been planted to create a windbreak. Because Elizabeth keeps bees, most of the plants are old cottage-type nectar or pollen producers; colour-themed beds include one devoted to hot yellows, reds and purples, another to blues, pinks and whites. You are welcome to stay all day in this paradise if you like – have a picnic just outside your room, then badger-watch in the evening. It is a gorgeous, peaceful spot. *Open garden for local charity.*

Details		Contact
• Rooms: 1 double, 1 twin/double. • Price: £70-£80. • Meals: Pub 2 miles. • Travel Club offer: 10% off stays Sunday-Thursday. • Ethical Collection: Food. See page 10.	**On your doorstep** • Whitton Churchyard: wild daffodils in March – idyllic • Stockton Bury Gardens: working farm & sheltered four-acre garden midst medieval buildings; no children/dogs; restaurant in the tithe barn **Top tip** Avoid slug pellets – keep Indian Runner ducks instead!	Elizabeth & David Hatchell The Croft Cottage B&B, Cumberley Lane, Knowbury, Ludlow SY8 3LJ 01584 890664 info@ludlow-breakfast.co.uk www.ludlow-breakfast.co.uk Map: see page 96

Acton Pigot

Two acres of shrubs, lawns & trees underplanted with bulbs & perennials

The house

From the double room with its hand-printed wallpaper and oak chests you look to Acton Burnell hill; England's first parliament was held here. The yellow room has views of lake, garden and Welsh hills; sunsets can be spectacular. Wooden doors, floors, carved settle and chests sit well with elegant furniture, fine prints and photographs. Happy in their role of hosts, the Owens spoil you with afternoon tea (most of it homemade) before a log fire. Parts of the house were built in 1660; the site is mentioned in the Domesday book. A restorative place run by lovely people.

The garden

Ferocious fecundity – as if the entire two-acre garden had been magically manured and then left to marinate. John's mother is a great gardener (if you want another treat ask to see her next-door paradise) and she laid out the structure. John and Hildegard have worked hard to bring it into line and the results are magnificent. Dividing the garden into sections the drive up to the house is heaving with huge euphorbias in raised aubretia-clad stone beds, there are thousands of bulbs, an iris bed, large shrubs planted through with ramblers and lovely giant yew balls for structure. The front garden is enclosed with a lawn (croquet in summer) and a huge late-flowering magnolia leans against the almost green house; the back section is all mixed borders with a walled garden by an old swimming pool where sun-lovers are planted. A vegetable, fruit and herb garden provides goodies for the kitchen. There are many rare shrubs and trees, and a wood for each of their three children. Scent is important, especially near the terrace – a wonderful spot for alfresco meals or simply sitting. The garden gently peters out with no boundary to open fields and a lake where ducks, geese, curlews and other water birds flap happily – go quietly and you will hear that lark rising. Hildegard says "you can't force nature" but she has done a jolly good persuading job.

Details

- Rooms: 1 double, 1 twin/double, 1 family room.
- Price: £80. Singles £50.
- Meals: Pub 3 miles.

On your doorstep
- The Dower House Garden, Morville Hall: highlights in every season, from June's roses to Sept's michaelmas daisies
- Long Mynd: heather moorland views, great for a hike

Top tip
Avoid disturbing the soil too much, or unearthed seeds will germinate into weeds

Contact

John & Hildegard Owen
Acton Pigot,
Acton Burnell, Shrewsbury SY5 7PH

01694 731209
07850 124000 (mobile)
actonpigot@farming.co.uk
www.actonpigot.co.uk

Map: see page 96

Yew Tree House

One-and-a-half acres of tranquillity & mystery – and Clive's fascinating sculptures

The house

A dreamy rurality in this much untrumpeted county, where the Montgomery canal makes its lazy way to Frankton Locks. One of Clive's huge sculptures greets you as you drive in to your neat, self-contained room with outside seating. These two contemporary, almost hotel-like spaces sport furniture of a highly functional modern design. Art peppers the walls, floors are bamboo with modern rugs, beds are hugely comfortable, bathrooms small and bang up to date. You eat well: breakfast on local dry-cure bacon or 'savoury duck' (contains no duck!). Clive and Jo are warm, easy-going souls.

The garden

A well-established garden – about one-and-a-half acres – of lawns, woodland, shrubbery, flower beds, pond and wildlife area, linked by lots of grassed paths. From your terrace you can walk past the herb garden; backed by a fence made of coloured poles, with sculptural spirals dotted through its beds, this is a quirky delight. Round the house you then come to a terrace with tables and chairs leading onto smooth lawns enclosed by trees, some rare (a tulip tree, a weeping ash), and deep beds packed with colour. There's a serene pond, a homemade Stonehenge, an orchard brimming with apple trees, living willow structures, a secluded arbour and an arch into a very special circle of grass surrounded by shrubs and with a flower bed at its centre. Everything within the circle is painted blue: the sculpture, the rose pyramids and the bench. There are two woodland areas, one in the main garden underplanted with spring bulbs and shade-tolerant perennials, the other recently planted as native Shropshire broadleaf woodland. The peace is broken only by birdsong and there are plenty of places to sit and ponder, but you are not alone; Clive's sculptures – some up to 15 feet tall – lurk round corners and peek from bushes. Lovely. *Open for Borderlands Visual Arts Open Studios.*

Details

- Rooms: 1 double, 1 twin/double.
- Price: £79-£90. Singles £59-£70.
- Meals: Pubs/restaurants nearby.

On your doorstep
- Chirk Castle: 18th-century park & 19th-century garden with clipped yews, big borders and, in Feb, carpets of snowdrops
- Shrewsbury Flower Show, mid-Aug: est. 1875!

Top tip
Feed the birds in winter & they will stay to eat your garden pests in summer

Contact

Clive & Jo Wilson
Yew Tree House,
Lower Frankton,
Oswestry SY11 4PB

01691 622126
info@yewtreebandb.co.uk
www.yewtreebandb.co.uk

Map: see page 96

Manor House

A garden for exploring but full of places to relax

The house

A working rare-breed farm in an area of great beauty, a Jacobean farmhouse with oodles of history. Behind mullioned windows is an interior crammed with curios and family pieces, panelled walls and wonky floors... hurl a log on the fire and watch it roar. Rooms with views have four-posters; one bathroom flaunts rich red antique fabrics. Chris and Margaret serve perfect breakfasts (home-grown tomatoes, sausages and bacon from their outdoor-reared pigs, eggs from their hens) and give you the run of the garden with tennis and croquet. There are two springer spaniels and one purring cat. Heaven.

The garden

When the house was rebuilt in 1708 the garden was devised. The house sits on a north-facing slope and the three-acre garden runs out on the south side into a series of five terraces, each one topped by neatly clipped yews. Chris inherited the house, then set to expand and improve the garden into a place of exploration, rest and relaxation; many seats are dotted here and there for lovely views over the Weaver hills. There is humour and quirk too: an extensive perennial border sports a huge stone table which was once part of the entrance to Lancaster's municipal baths, and an old goods railway carriage is now a garden summerhouse. Yew trees, hedge walls and terraces mean that you have to wander to see the full value of the garden, and guests are encouraged to stay as long as they want. Planting includes lots of evergreens with splashes of summer colour, and the odd pretty weed – Chris will brook no spraying at all. This means the wildlife is abundant, from birds and butterflies to hedgehogs and squirrels. The old cow lane is now a mown path, and remains of old farm buildings have been left covered with ivy and with statues placed among them. A lovely, interesting garden filled with fun, and very peaceful to sit in.

Details

- Rooms: 4 doubles.
- Price: £58-£75. Singles £38-£48.
- Meals: Pub/restaurant 1.5 miles.
- Travel Club offer: 10% off room rate Mon-Thurs.
- Ethical Collection: Food. See page 10.

On your doorstep
- Consall Hall Gardens: 70 acres of landscaped idyll; lakes, follies & bridges blend with conservation efforts to create a garden that changes beautifully with the seasons
- Hopton Hall: snowdrops & aconites in Feb

Top tip
Don't be too eager to pull out pretty flowering weeds

Contact

Chris & Margaret Ball
Manor House, Prestwood,
Denstone, Uttoxeter ST14 5DD

01889 590415
07976 767629 (mobile)
cm_ball@yahoo.co.uk
towersabovetherest.com

Map: see page 96

Bents Farmhouse

An English country garden sweet
with flowers & peaceful corners

The house

You're looked after impeccably here: Jill gives you
breakfasts of local sausages and bacon, smoked
salmon and scrambled eggs, pancakes if you'd love
them, all served when you like and in the garden in
summer. At tea time there are homemade cakes and
biscuits, so it's just as well you have your own
sitting room with open fire to snooze in. Your
bedroom is large, light, romantic and elegant with a
balcony overlooking the garden; the bathroom is
just along (your own) corridor and has a claw-foot
bath. There are good pubs within strolling distance
and lovely walks. Peaceful.

The garden

There wasn't a plant in the garden when Jill moved in – just a large expanse of lawn, some ugly conifers and, luckily, an ancient yew tree. Whoosh forward a couple of decades to find a beautiful, naturalistic English country garden surrounding the house on three sides and packed with roses, each chosen for its individual beauty and fragrance by garden designer Jill. The largest part of the garden is to the side of the house: find a wisteria-covered pergola, a lavender walk, semi-circular herbaceous beds, wildflowers, a pond, sculptures, and a dazzling display of old and English roses. Dotted about are tables and chairs with pretty floral cushions; keep following the sun around and you'll find serene corners to read in, or just sky to watch. Potter over to the vegetable garden with its low picket fence, gravelled path, rose-covered arbour and abundant soft fruits and salads. Jill's passion for nature means her roses are grown without chemicals, and her love of birds is evident: there are goldfinches, greenfinches, long-tailed tits and woodpeckers. At the front of the house are four beautiful pink ornamental cherries; at dusk you can watch the colony of bats show off their acrobatic skills. A delight all round. *NGS, RHS.*

Details		Contact
• Rooms: 1 double. • Price: £95. Singles £70. • Meals: Pubs/restaurants 5-minute walk. • Travel Club offer: Bottle of champagne for bookings of 2 nights or more. Late checkout (12pm).	**On your doorstep** • Coton Manor: magical five-acre bluebell wood, & a colourful wildflower meadow at its best June/July • Kelmarsh Hall: joyful summer borders, & snowdrops in Feb **Top tip** Plant native flowers in your borders to encourage bees & butterflies	Jill Mackenzie Bents Farmhouse, Church Drive, Gilmorton LE17 5PF 01455 558566 fourseasons@harborough.uk.com www.fourseasonsgardendesign.com Map: see page 96

Westfield

An enclosed half-acre packed with 1,500 plant species, shrubs and trees

The house

The surprises come thick and fast. First, after an unexceptional approach, the charm of the village. Then, behind a modern entrance, a rambling period house, once two cottages. One, 18th-century and stone, has flagstone floors and its original pump; the other, Victorian and brick, has been joined to an outbuilding by an extension so that its Aga-warmed kitchen and living area seem almost part of the garden. Bedrooms are traditional, comfortable and have tea trays with bone china. Be welcomed by wonderful, down-to-earth people – this is a delightful place to stay and great value.

The garden

When Colin and Vicky arrived here 39 years ago, the half-acre garden was a random forest of native trees. Drastic culling helped to give much-needed structure: they left a few indigenous trees and planted ornamental species (Indian bean tree, liquidambar, ponderosa pine, black walnut). Then they set about creating three separate areas. The result is a meandering, engaging garden, completely surrounded by high walls or impenetrable hedge, which is stunning in spring, summer and autumn. Shrubs – philadelphus, weigelia, deutzia – mass together and deep borders glow with rare French irises, day lilies, penstemon or superb hellebores.

The collection of unusual plants is growing all the time. Beside the new extension is a terrace which drops away to three walled areas with more beds and a weeping pear tree. Emma, Vicky's mother, came to live with them some years ago and is obviously a presiding genius. Her pride and joy is the Victorian greenhouse, where she cherishes rare scented geraniums, jasmines and orchids. She is always changing, moving and finding better and more interesting species. All three share and love this garden, so it's a real pleasure to visit. *RHS.*

Details		Contact
• Rooms: 2 twins/doubles. • Price: £60. Singles £35. • Meals: Pubs/restaurants 10-minute walk. • Travel Club offer: Garden tour for plant lovers. Advice on propagation, growing, pruning. Seedlings when available.	**On your doorstep** • Cottesbrook Hall: outstanding gardens & the famous Plant Finders Fair in June • Coton Manor: English country garden with wonderful Rose Bank & a nursery that promotes natural predators & nematodes **Top tip** No two gardens are the same & all require individual care	C B Mynott Westfield, 36 Main Road, Crick, Northampton NN6 7TX 01788 822313 cbm@mynott.com Map: see page 96

Hambleton Hall Hotel

Lovely south-facing terraced gardens with spectacular lake views

The house

A sublime country house, one of the loveliest in England, on a tiny peninsular jutting into Rutland Water. Sail, cycle or walk around it, then return to squishy sofas by the fire in the panelled hall, a pillared bar in red for cocktails, and French windows opening to delightful gardens. The bedrooms are the very best – hand-stitched Italian linen, mirrored armoires, marble bathrooms and faultless fabrics. The Croquet Pavilion, a deeply comfortable two-bedroom suite, has its own terrace. Polish the day off with incredible food: there's a Michelin star in the dining room.

The garden

The winding drive is engulfed by mature limes, cedars, beeches and oak. Owner Tim, who taught himself tree surgery, has added cork oaks, holm oaks, a strawberry tree and *Pinus pinea* among others. He and Stefa inherited the garden in 1979 and it is now idyllic, with a fine south-facing terrace overlooking a formal parterre and spectacular views of Rutland Water beyond. A host of snowdrops, aconites and tulips (Tim dislikes daffodils) herald the spring, followed by flowering shrubs, roses and foliage plants, interspersed with crisply clipped yew, box and evergreen oaks for architectural interest in winter. To the left of the hall is a steeply banked garden surrounding the Pavilion Room, mainly laid to lawns that lead through fields towards the lake; behind a high hedge is a croquet lawn. Anyone for tennis? Dive down the stunning wisteria walk for a set or two, then admire the fecund fruit and vegetable garden with its neat raised beds, fruit cages and beautiful Victorian greenhouses; all is destined for the table. Ruminate on one of the many stone and wooden benches tucked into the trees and shrubbery, or float in the outdoor heated pool. Gorgeous.

Details

- Rooms: 16 twins/doubles. Pavilion: 1 suite for 4.
- Price: £225-£390. Singles £190. Pavilion £525-£625.
- Meals: Continental b'fast included; full English £17. Lunch from £22. Dinner £38-£70.
- Travel Club offer: Bottle of champagne for bookings of 2 nights or more. Late checkout (12pm).

On your doorstep
- Barnsdale Gardens: originally the work of Geoff Hamilton, a collection of 38 individually designed & meticulously labelled plots, an inspiration for small gardens

Top tip
Views should tease: never reveal all at the beginning of the show!

Contact

Tim & Stefa Hart
Hambleton Hall Hotel,
Ketton Road, Hambleton,
Oakham LE15 8TH

01572 756991
hotel@hambletonhall.com
www.hambletonhall.com

Map: see page 96

Kelling House

Charming cottage garden full of secret places & unexpected surprises

The house

Dating from 1785, three old cottages are now a long, low, rose-covered house of gentle rubble stone with a pantile roof, a pretty painted gate edged with lolling hollyhocks and a super garden. Well-proportioned rooms have good English furniture, well-made thick curtains and interesting paintings; the creamy sitting room overlooks the quiet street on one side and the garden on the other. Bedrooms are softly coloured with a pretty mix of checks, stripes and plain white cotton. Sue is delightful and looks after you without fuss, breakfast will set you up for the day.

The garden

When Sue arrived in 1999 she kept only a few good shrubs and mature trees; the rest she bulldozed. Now French windows and doors lead directly onto the generous flagged terrace with its young box-edged parterre filled with herbs. Clumps of lavender, rosemary and sage give a Mediterranean feel and scent the house but it is also a lovely place to sit and admire the rest – in particular, the wide bed of summer-flowering perennials: sweet-scented white phlox, elegant perovskia with its lavender blue spikes and grey foliage, and dramatic acanthus. From here the lawn runs to the southern boundary, while a curving herbaceous border softens the eastern boundary and leads to a small area of young ornamental trees. The western beds reveal tulip and walnut trees interspersed with shrubs and grasses. This is a young garden but it's charming and well planted with good lawns and unexpected surprises that invite inspection... there are interesting small trees and flowering shrubs that include grey-leafed cistus, santolina and rue. In summer, colours are pink, white and blue. Belvoir Castle is worth visiting – as are the magnificent cathedrals of Lincoln and Peterborough.

Photographs © Paul Sands

Details

- Rooms: 2 doubles, 1 single.
- Price: £75. Singles from £45.
- Meals: Dinner, by arrangement, £25. Packed lunch £7.50. Pub/restaurant 3-minute walk.

On your doorstep
- Belton House: lakeside walks (BBC's Pride & Prejudice) are a pleasure for would-be Elizabeth Bennets
- Easton Walled Gardens: 12 acres of 'lost' 400-year-old gardens undergoing revival

Top tip
To preserve roses, hold cut stems over a candle for 10 seconds & put into deep, cold water

Contact

Sue Evans
Kelling House, 17 West Street,
Barkston, Grantham NG32 2NL

01400 251440
07771 761251 (mobile)
sue.evans7@btinternet.com
www.kellinghouse.co.uk

Map: see page 96

Lincolnshire

Baumber Park

Sensuous planting & unhindered views for peace & inspiration

The house

Lincoln red cows and Longwool sheep surround this attractive farmhouse. The old watering pond is now a haven for frogs, newts and toads, birds sing lustily, Maran hens conjure delicious eggs and charming Clare, a botanist, is knowledgeable about the area. Bedrooms are large light and traditional with mahogany furniture; two have heart-stopping views over the garden to farmland. Guests have their own entrance, sitting room with a log fire and dining room with local books. Good walking, riding and cycling country, with quiet lanes. *Min. two nights at weekends in high season.*

The garden

If I were a bird I would go and live in this garden. Just over an acre of delicious smelling flowers, shrubs and hedges (sea buckthorn because the thrushes like the berries). "Scent is the thing," says Clare and even her favourite daffodil, 'Pheasant's Eye', smells lovely. Follow a formal gravel front bordered by lonicera hedges, under a solid pergola over which golden hop and honeysuckle battle for the sky, to lawn and large borders full of sweet-smelling roses, elaeagnus, buddleia, sedum and a maturing pocket handkerchief tree – planted to commemorate an anniversary! A box parterre has been created in the vegetable garden and beds are full, colourful and scented –

thousands of bulbs pop up in the spring. There's a vast cherry tree underplanted with more bulbs, periwinkles and holly, a peony bed interplanted with sweet-smelling viburnum, and then a lovely whitebeam arch through which peeps a wildflower meadow. Few large trees have been planted so views are un-hindered and an old pond is planted around with native species only – for the wildlife, lucky things. A small quantity of interesting plants are for sale – propagated by Clare. *Trustee of Lincolnshire Wildlife Trust; garden occasionally open for local charities & events.*

Details		Contact

Details

- Rooms: 2 doubles, 1 twin.
- Price: £62–£66. Singles from £35.
- Meals: Pubs 1.5 miles.
- Travel Club offer: Home-grown produce, as in season and available.
- Use your Sawday's Gift Card here.

On your doorstep
- Hatton Meadows: glorious old English meadow – plus butterflies
- Goltho Gardens: decisive planting gives strong colour, form & foliage; superb plants are propagated & sold onsite

Top tip
Don't let overgrown shrubs spoil the view: start again with cuttings or suckers

Contact

Clare Harrison
Baumber Park,
Baumber, Horncastle LN9 5NE

01507 578235
07977 722776 (mobile)
mail@baumberpark.com
www.baumberpark.com

Map: see page 96

Ashdene

A family of ten gardens in one
– with damask roses & touches
of humour

The house

A mile west of bustling Southwell and its lovely Minster, this big, light-filled family house dates from 1520. David and Glenys have packed it with wonderful paintings, samplers, embroidery, books on history and travel, old rugs and comfortable furniture. Guests have their drawing room with open fire, and you are spoiled at breakfast with home-baked bread, eggs from their hens, delicious jams. Bedrooms are gorgeous: pretty white bed linen, spotless bathrooms with fluffy towels and relaxing colours. Birdwatchers will be transfixed – but it's a short walk to an excellent pub.

The garden

An imaginative, really special garden in which both David and Glenys have worked very hard: their current project is a Bible garden in which they have planted fig, star of Bethlehem, angel's trumpets and sage among others. A gravel and boulder garden tucked around the front of the house has scented plants for spring and autumn, two huge yews have been cut to tall stumps, then their later sproutings coaxed and designed by David – one into a spiral, the other into a witty Rastafarian topknot. There's a white spring garden and a woodland walk along serpentine brick paths with precisely coppiced hazels. A long grass walk up a slope takes you away from the house and is edged with hornbeam – have a rest at the top, a favourite quiet spot. There are over 50 species of damask roses, paths through brick-raised beds of mixed planting and a central circle of five pillars around an Ali Baba urn. The vegetable garden is fecund but neat, the sunken garden and the terrace by the house have good seating areas. David's topiary is artistic and striking – so this is what retired surgeons do! Their use of chemical help with all this? None. An organic garden which attracts many birds (38 nests at the last count) and a centuries-old colony of bees. *NGS, RHS. Open for garden clubs & charities.*

Details

- Rooms: 2 doubles, 1 twin, 1 single.
- Price: £70. Singles £50.
- Meals: Pub 4-minute walk.
- Travel Club offer: Free pick-up from local bus/train station. 10% off room rate Mon-Thurs.
- Ethical Collection: Community; Food. See page 10.

On your doorstep
- Sherwood Forest: stumble upon an 800-year-old oak in the heart of ancient woodland, reputed haunt of Robin Hood
- Hollybeck Nurseries: high-quality plants for sale – buy Lincolnshire-grown shrubs & David Austin roses

Top tip
Leave seed heads on perennials for the birds during winter

Contact

David Herbert
Ashdene,
Halam,
Southwell NG22 8AH

01636 812335
david@herbert.newsurf.net

Map: see page 96

Derbyshire

Horsleygate Hall

Inspiring garden with artistic surprises & superb kitchen garden

The house

The Fords have an eye for finding old treasures and recycled items, and putting them in the perfect place: this is more shabby than chic and all the better for it. Find worn kilims on stone flags, striped and floral wallpapers, comfy sofas, underwhelming but spotless bathrooms and the integrity of the building undisturbed: there's a warm and timeless feel. The setting is stunning – on a hillside with views of moors, trees, fields and very little else. Food is nearly all from the garden and homemade: bread, jam, fruit, veg and eggs from the hens. *Children over five welcome.*

The garden

Margaret and Robert are dedicated, skilful, knowledgeable gardeners and their talents are abundantly clear from the moment you arrive. Margaret is a true plantsman who knows and loves her plants; Robert is the garden architect. He has added delightful touches, including a pergola fashioned from the iron pipes of the old greenhouse heating system, a breeze house thatched in Yorkshire heather and fences made from holly poles. Exploring the garden is enormous fun – there are so many surprises. The sloping site includes a woodland garden with gazebo, hot sun terrace, rockeries, pools, a fern area, a jungle garden, mixed borders and an exquisite ornamental kitchen garden. The Fords are keen on evergreen shrubs and have an interest in euphorbias. They have a particularly unusual collection of herbaceous perennials and are always on the lookout for fresh treasures to add to their collection. Quirky statuary peeps out at you from unusual places and all around the garden are strategically placed seats where you can soak up the varied displays. The overall theme is one of informality, with walls, terraces, paths and well-planted troughs hidden from each other. Lovely in spring, gorgeous in the full flower of summer, and good for autumn colour and winter interest, too. *NGS.*

Details

- Rooms: 1 double, 1 twin, 1 family room.
- Price: £70-£80. Singles from £50.
- Meals: Pub/restaurant 1 mile.
- Travel Club offer: 5% off stays of 2 or more nights.

On your doorstep
- Renishaw Hall: imaginative planting, both geometric & naturalistic
- Chatsworth House: rose, cottage & kitchen gardens, famous fountains & walks in 105 ever-changing acres

Top tip
Be sure to research new plants thoroughly before planting

Contact

Robert & Margaret Ford
Horsleygate Hall,
Horsleygate Lane,
Holmesfield S18 7WD

01142 890333

Map: see page 96

The Croft

An organic country garden,
a little haven of bounty
- with hens

The house

What a surprise! Hidden behind trees in serious
suburbia is a charming Arts & Crafts house with a
smart front door; attentive Sandra may greet you
with her own delicious scones and blackcurrant jam.
The entrance hall has a gleaming oak floor and
vases of fresh flowers. Most of the Deco features are
retained: an extraordinary copper fireplace in the
sitting room and wonderful patterned windows. In
the bedrooms Shaker meets subtle chintz with
stripped floors, painted furniture and a splash of
gingham here and there; bathrooms are ultra
modern. Just ten minutes from the airport.

The garden

A lovely, relaxed garden packed full of cottage favourites and not at all in keeping with the suburban surroundings. Sandra and Rick have lived here for over 25 years and their organic garden has evolved with them. From the house there is a large south-facing lawn overlooked by a veranda, a vine-covered terrace and a raised terrace surrounded by bamboo and honeysuckle; enjoy an evening drink or a cup of tea here – or choose one of the several benches dotted about the garden. There's a pretty, box-edged parterre filled with salad and herbs, steps lead down to the wilder bottom garden with a pond and reclaimed greenhouse where Rick sows his seeds for the following year; Sandra designs and does the weeding and harvesting – cut flowers for the house and sweet peas every year. It is all highly productive; a small orchard area provides fruit for homemade jams, and the organic vegetable garden yields much for the table. Mature trees – copper beech, conifers and silver birch – are home to plenty of birds and wildlife. It's all so peaceful you would never imagine Manchester was so close. *RHS, occasionally open for charity.*

Details

- Rooms: 2 doubles.
- Price: £80. Singles £65.
- Meals: Restaurant 500 yards.
- Travel Club offer: Glass of champagne on arrival.

On your doorstep
- Hare Hill Gardens: charming wooded & walled garden surrounded by parkland, very fine in early summer
- Peover Gardens: pleached limes, roses & a lily pool; visit in May/June for azaleas & rhododendrons

Top tip
Don't be over pristine: be wildlife friendly. The rewards are fascinating

Contact

Sandra Megginson
The Croft,
Wilmslow SK9 6LZ

01625 523435
07866 242010 (mobile)
thecroftbedandbreakfast@yahoo.co.uk
www.thecroftbedandbreakfastwilmslow.co.uk

Map: see page 96

Lancashire • Cumbria • Yorkshire • Northumberland

England: The North

England: The North

Special places to stay

The Ridges

Sheltered orchard garden with cottage planting, formal lawns & woodland walk

The house

John and Barbara look after you in a lovely old mill-owner's house built in the 1700s. Traditional bedrooms are upstairs with pale colours, flowery fabrics, patterned walls and wrought-iron beds; breakfast is downstairs in a cosy room overlooking the garden, with a log-burner for chilly mornings. Ornaments and pictures abound. The magnificent West Pennine Moors are great for walkers and cyclists: the energetic can brave the Commonwealth Games Course, pootlers can amble along the woods and reservoirs below the Pike. Both garden and welcome will delight you.

The garden

The story of Barbara's garden starts in the 1970s when she used to help her mother with their garden centre. The more she learned, the more her interest grew: by the time her children had grown and flown she was hooked. Realising the potential of the garden, she began restoring and developing. The old apple trees lining the path were pruned, but not much else is recognisable now; instead, dense cottage garden planting demonstrates Barbara's eye for combinations of colour, form and foliage. Through a living arch, a lawned area is fringed with bright foliaged specimen trees cleverly positioned to shine against dark copper beech, holly and rhododendron. This shelter protects such tender plants as windmill palm and *Magnolia grandiflora*: a lovely setting for a Victorian-style glass house used for entertaining. In a natural looking stream garden damp-loving plants such as rodgersia and gunnera grow down towards a pool, while a 'Paul's Himalayan Musk' runs rampant over trellis and trees. An old buttressed wall has been uncovered to create a new, naturally planted quiet area, with scented plants and herbs to attract butterflies and bees. Let Barbara take you on a tour: the history is fascinating. *NGS, Good Gardens Guide.*

Details

- Rooms: 2 doubles, 1 twin/double, 1 single.
- Price: From £70. Singles £40.
- Meals: Pub within walking distance.
- Travel Club offer: 10% off room rate.

On your doorstep
- Hoghton Tower: Elizabethan manor with fine grounds, a formal rose garden, sunken garden, ornamental yews - and a farmers' market the 3rd Sunday of the month

Top tip
Place chicken wire over tall perennials & raise as the plant grows

Contact

John & Barbara Barlow
The Ridges,
Weavers Brow, Limbrick,
Chorley PR6 9EB

01257 279981
barbara@barlowridges.co.uk
www.bedbreakfast-gardenvisits.com

Map: see page 188

Cumbria

Barn Close

Wildlife-friendly two acres looking to the landscape beyond

The house

There's a lovely atmosphere here; peaceful, unpretentious, relaxed. Anne is cheerful and energetic and gives you lots of personal attention in her 1920s house in the village with lots of windows, high chimneys and well-proportioned rooms off long and spacious corridors. Bedrooms (the main room is much bigger) are traditional and comfortable; bathrooms (not huge) have baths and showers. Suppers at the mahogany table are by arrangement and will include home-grown vegetables. Excellent value, and perfect for bird lovers, walkers and those who love a bit of cossetting.

The garden

A delightful two-acre garden with something to interest the garden lover at any time of the year. Wonderful displays of snowdrops, aconites and bluebells in spring, a swathe of autumn colour from the surrounding mature trees, and a large herbaceous border that's stunning in June and July. Mike organises birdwatching breaks around the local area but you need not go very far: over the last ten years nearly 80 different species have been seen from or in the garden. Anne has planted teasels, acanthus, grasses and anything with seedheads to attract the birds but, needless to say, they are equally keen on her productive vegetable garden and fruit trees. The pond has been supplemented with water irises, candelabra primulas and water lilies: wildlife flourishes, particularly dragonflies, and a good number of resident butterflies. This is a beautiful unspoiled part of Cumbria (AONB), with lovely views and good walks round Morecambe Bay, famous for its huge flocks of wading birds. There are many places of interest nearby including Levens Hall, Sizergh Castle (NT) and Holker Hall, while the Lakeland Horticultural Society garden is a gem overlooking Lake Windermere. The plant centre in the village, Beetham Nurseries, won a much coveted gold medal at the Tatton RHS show 2008. *RHS, HPS, Lakeland Horticultural Society, Cumbria Gardens Trust.*

Details

- Rooms: 2 twins, 1 single.
- Price: £45-£70. Singles £28-£45.
- Meals: Supper £20.
  Light bites from £10. Pub 300 yards.

On your doorstep
- Levens Hall: a garden in its original 1694 design; stately topiary & glorious underplanting
- Sizergh Castle: medieval castle with hardy fern & limestone rock garden

Top tip
Find out what soil type you have to give your plants the best start

Contact

Anne Robinson
Barn Close,
Beetham LA7 7AL

01539 563191
07752 670658 (mobile)
anne@nwbirds.co.uk
www.nwbirds.co.uk/bcindex.htm

Map: see page 188

Broadgate

A garden developed by the family over 200 years, with a wonderful estuary view

The house

Through white stone pillars is a lovely Georgian house facing south, with stunning views down to the sea. Guests have the whole of the third floor to themselves: gorgeous flowery bedrooms with high, comfortable beds and pretty mahogany furniture, most facing east for sunny mornings. There's a little sitting room and a breakfast room with floor-to-ceiling, china-filled cupboards. Diana is an accomplished cook who treats you to home-produced vegetables and fruits. Walking starts from the door, up to the bracing fells or down to the bird-filled estuary. *Children over ten welcome.*

The garden

This is a classic Cumbrian country house garden, 300 years old, complete with stone balustrade and planters, box garden and fragrant roses, venerable trees and lashings of rhododendron and azalea. With the spring come wave upon wave of snowdrops (2,500 were planted last spring) and merry daffodils. A walled garden, engagingly faded in its woodland setting, tells of gardeners and summers long ago. High stone walls, covered with climbers and old roses, enclose wide herbaceous beds and an old glasshouse. At the front of the house, vivid 'Greek' blue hydrangeas make a startling contrast to the white façade and smooth green lawns, while an old palm tree adds an exotic touch. This is a garden in the most wonderful setting and which Diana constantly adds to for year-round interest; its bones are good and there are lots of paths to follow, places to sit and dream, and wildlife to watch. In winter there are ponies in the field, and masses of birdlife, too, including flycatchers and green woodpeckers. Down the lane are some interesting old buildings belonging to the estate farm, where chickens peck under the trees and cattle graze. *Open for church, garden & historical groups.*

Details

- Rooms: 2 doubles, 2 singles.
- Price: £90. Singles £55.
- Meals: Dinner, 3 courses, £25. Pub 5 miles.
- Travel Club offer: Bottle of wine with dinner on first night. Late checkout (12pm). Canapés and glass of wine before dinner.

On your doorstep
- Muncaster Castle: catch sensational rhododendrons & azaleas in April/June
- Swinside Stone Circle: a short walk up the fell to a stunning backdrop – visit on the winter or summer solstice

Top tip
Dead-head hydrangeas at the end of March & cut back all dead wood

Contact

Diana Lewthwaite
Broadgate,
Millom,
Broughton-in-Furness LA18 5JY

01229 716295
dilewthwaite@bghouse.co.uk
www.broadgate-house.co.uk

Map: see page 188

Gilpin Hotel & Lake House

Twenty acres of gardens, woodland & wildflower meadow - natural simplicity

The house

Run to perfection by two generations of the same family, Gilpin delivers at every turn. Clipped country-house elegance flows throughout: smouldering coals, Zoffany wallpaper, gilded mirrors, flowers everywhere. Bedrooms have exquisite fabrics, delicious art; some with French windows that open onto the garden, others with hot tubs on private terraces, all have sofas or armchairs. Further afield the Lake House suites are deeply plush, one with a glass wall overlooking Knipe Tarn; a car will whisk you to the restaurant and back again in the evenings for delicious suppers.

The garden

Up at the main house you're in 20 acres of silence, so throw open doors and sit on the south-facing (and candlelit) terrace surrounded by pots of colour. Or stroll through the different garden rooms for magnolias, cherry blossom and a fine copper beech as well as the odd pond. The South Garden was planted by Great Grandmother Cunliffe in 1917: largely Victorian in style, the sweeping lawns are laid with borders and hedgerows with mature trees including brightly coloured acers, camellias and rhododendrons. The East Garden has lawns and borders that rise up the hill, a water feature, and a rockery of Japanese heathers. Just a mile away is the Lake House with stunning all-round views: once simple grazing land it is now idyllic woodland that blends seamlessly into the landscape. A rockery winds up to a Druid circle and the kitchen garden has pristine beds of raised slate. New herbaceous gardens lead to another woodland garden and a trail which winds round the lake; a clearing in the woods reveals dramatic glimpses down the Lyth valley and to Morecambe Bay. Laze on the jetty with a book and listen to nought but birds.

Details

- Rooms: 8 doubles, 12 twins/doubles, 6 suites.
- Price: Half-board £290-£600. Singles from £180.
- Meals: Lunch £10-£35. Dinner included.
- Travel Club offer: Champagne afternoon tea on day of arrival.

On your doorstep
- Levens Hall: imagine yourself Alice in Wonderland as topiary towers above you
- Holehird Gardens: ten-acre hillside garden in gorgeous Lakeland setting with alpine greenhouses

Top tip
Recycle all window box bulbs to the gardens – we go through at least 1,600 a year!

Contact

John, Christine, Barnaby & Zoe Cunliffe
Gilpin Hotel & Lake House, Crook Road, Windermere LA23 3NE

015394 88818
hotel@gilpinlodge.co.uk
www.gilpinlodge.co.uk

Map: see page 188

Spooney Green

A verdant cottage garden created
with love & shared with pleasure

The house

Heart-lifting views – down the long garden, across
the invisible road and to the hills. The traffic hum is
quickly forgotten in the comfortable house with a
strong pine theme. There is no sitting room and you
breakfast at two separate tables, but on a sunny day
you may sit in the garden for hours, and soak up the
enthusiasms of Sandra and Ian. Sleep in simple,
comfortable, unpretentious bedrooms – a massive
relief to the walkers who lope down the great
Skiddaw hill right behind. Stoke up on homemade
muesli, home-baked bread from locally milled flour,
and Ian's potato cakes – delicious.

The garden

Sandra and Ian's greatest love is the natural world. In nine years they have created a magical garden out of what was just boggy fields; now the basic plan is to create more formal gardens around the house, moving down through bog area, the pond and then on into a wildflower meadow. Another area has been set aside for a productive fruit and vegetable garden, and for Sandra's beehives. Secluded spaces have been created to sit and enjoy the bird and animal life that now abounds. Terraces at the front of the house face south and are a peaceful place to enjoy the stunning views of the western Lake District fells. Flower beds are crammed with cottage garden favourites, which attract bees and other pollinating insects. An ancient lime tree is in full flower in July and the lime honey produced will find its way to your breakfast table. This committed couple garden organically and enjoy eating what they produce: soft fruits for jams and for breakfast in season, eggs from their hens, honey from the hives. If they are not out walking or birdwatching you will find them in the garden; not a day goes by without one of them having a 'good idea' – and they sell surplus plants. *NGS.*

Details		Contact

• Rooms: 3 doubles.
• Price: £75. Singles £60.
• Meals: Packed lunch £5.
  Pub/restaurant 500 yards.
	On your doorstep
	• Rannerdale: ancient battlefield
	  displays a glorious April carpet of
	  bluebells
	• Mirehouse: Scots pines planted in
	  1784 line the drive, softened by
	  pretty flowers & a bee garden
	
	Top tip
	Cut the sides of wild hedges on
	alternate years to leave winter
	berries for birds
		Sandra Wallace
		Spooney Green,
		Spooney Green Lane,
		Keswick CA12 4PJ
		
		01768 772601
		spooneygreen@tiscali.co.uk
		
		Map: see page 188

Austwick Hall

Luscious gardens & woodland trail
in the Yorkshire Dales National Park

The house

This grand old manor house has a Tudor door,
a Georgian porch and may have started life as a
12th-century pele tower. Today it's a rather lovely,
intimate hotel with rugs on a flagstone floor, sofas
in front of the wood-burner, a vase of flowers on a
rosewood table and a butterfly staircase that leads
to pretty grand bedrooms; some are big, others are
huge and the simplest is quite divine, with a golden
four-poster and garden views. There's colour,
exceptional art and a half-panelled dining room for
fabulous food. The Dales are for walking, Kirkby
Lonsdale is close for antiques.

The garden

The garden's original structure probably dates from late Georgian times. Old features (an impressive sundial) and trees (the woodland was planted in the 1800s) sit in easy harmony alongside Michael and Eric's more recent developments which include a sculpture trail, a contemporary knot garden and a walled vegetable garden which supplies the kitchen. There are 13 glorious acres in all, the mature woodland flaunts the finest specimen Atlantic blue cedar and a collection of giant redwoods; a series of terraces wrap themselves around the house; and long herbaceous borders flank the main lawn and blaze with colour all summer. Gravel walkways link interesting garden 'rooms': take a stroll down the stately juniper walk to the deliciously wild jungle garden or laze about in the heather-thatched gazebo or the pretty pergola with throne-like chairs. The couple have successfully repatriated the Austwick Hall fern collection from the Fibrex nursery (it dates from Victorian times), planted over 120,000 bulbs, and are actively enhancing the biodiversity of the woodland: listen out for woodpeckers drumming and owls hooting. Best of all is the stunning snowdrop and sculpture walk, with 41 varieties on display from January to March. Special. *NGS, RHS.*

Details

- Rooms: 4 doubles, 1 suite.
- Price: £145-£175.
  Singles £110-£160.
- Meals: Dinner, 5 courses, £35.
  Packed lunch £5.
- Travel Club offer: Bottle of wine with dinner on first night.

On your doorstep
- Gresgarth Hall: gardens flanking the Artle Beck lavishly planted with new interest each season (hamamelis in Feb, hellebores in March); check open days

Top tip
Snowdrops are most successful when lifted as dormant bulbs, as late as May; replant before they get dry

Contact

Michael Pearson & Eric Culley
Austwick Hall,
Town Head, Austwick,
Lancaster LA2 8BS

01524 251794
austwickhall@austwick.org
www.austwickhall.co.uk

Map: see page 188

Cold Cotes

A garden at ease in its rural setting
- full of interest & mass plantings

The house

Ed and Penny give you peace and quiet and a dollop of chic in their 1890s farmhouse on the edge of the Yorkshire Dales. A sitting room with creamy walls, squashy sofas, roaring fire and loads of books is covered in Ed's paintings. The light, long dining room has a sprung floor should you need to dance; tuck in to homemade cakes for tea, local sausages for breakfast, and home-cooked suppers if you don't want to budge. Bedrooms have pale walls, fine fabrics, brass beds and roomy bathrooms; those in the converted barn are just as lovely, one with its own little kitchen area.

The garden

What was a five-acre field, facing a dominant westerly, has been shaken up royally! It is now a series of dazzling 'zones' starting next to the house with a stone-flagged terrace with clumps of thrift, miniature geraniums, euphorbias and pots of blue agapanthus. In front is a red bed made up of oriental poppies, dahlias, tulips and penstemon, then stone steps down to a formal garden. Golden hops scrabble over an obelisk, a pond is surrounded by sunny herb beds and hedging breaks it up into sections. Another hot bed is around the corner, a woodland walk is planted with cherry, sorbus, beech, alders and oak and there are some impressive sweeping borders inspired by the designer Piet Oudolf and containing his beloved prairie plants and grasses. A cobblestone walk (Penny Lane) ambles along a stream with a little bridge, planted around with gunnera, periwinkle, ivy and comfrey, leading to a thriving pond. A fruit and veg garden provides abundant produce; a little lawned area is surrounded by cherry trees and has a perfect seating area with old wooden furniture. A new garden focusing on shade lovers in a woodland setting is in its first exciting season; a circular wooded walk with naturalistic planting is in preparation. A garden for quiet contemplation, filled with birdsong. *NGS, open to the public last Sunday in August & by appointment.*

Details

- Rooms: 4 doubles, 2 twins/doubles (2 with own sitting rooms).
- Price: £70-£95.
- Meals: Light bites & supper by arrangement. Pub/restaurant 2.5 miles.
- Travel Club offer: 2 plants of your choice from our nursery.

On your doorstep
- Harlow Carr: blending into the landscape, one of the RHS's four showpiece gardens with some uniquely courageous planting, conscientiously supporting its wildlife

Top tip
Cut back perennials & grasses in spring to prepare winter shelter & food for birds

Contact

Ed Loft
Cold Cotes,
Felliscliffe,
Harrogate HG3 2LW

01423 770937
info@coldcotes.com
www.coldcotes.com

Map: see page 188

Photographs © Suzie Gibbons

Shallowdale House

Two acres of informal hillside garden with glorious views

The house

Phillip and Anton have a true affection for their guests so you will be treated like angels in small-hotel style. Sumptuous bedrooms dazzle in yellows, blues and limes, acres of curtains frame wide views over the Howardian Hills, bathrooms gleam. Breakfast on the best – fresh fruit compote, dry-cured bacon, homemade rolls – then walk it off in any direction from the door. Return to an elegant drawing room with a fire in winter, and an enticing library. Dinner is out of this world and coffee and chocolates all you need before you crawl up to bed. *Min. two nights at weekends.*

The garden

Keep climbing and by the time you get to the top of these two very lush acres you will feel you've had a country hike... so perch on a bench and drink in the Yorkshire air. The many specimen trees planted when the house was built 40-odd years ago are growing up beautifully. Weeping birch, cypress, cherry, maple, acer and copper beech hover over swathes of grass underplanted with thousands of bulbs, a double rockery groans with scented shrubs like viburnum, rosemary and choisya; cistus, hardy geraniums, ceanothus, fuchsias and potentilla are popped in for colour. Lose yourself in the landscape – a lovely park-like atmosphere prevails – and sit and soak up the peace. Nearer the house there are more formal beds, a mini-orchard, a sunny terrace with tinkling water and clematis and roses that romp over the arches... mixed planting everywhere but in such good taste. Much discussion is of future projects and what to tackle next; hard work for just the two of them but Anton never goes up, or down, the hill without an armful of dead-heads and flotsam. Come for views which sweep from the Pennines to the Wolds.

Details

- Rooms: 1 double, 1 twin/double.
- Price: £97.50-£120.
  Singles £77.50-£95.
- Meals: Dinner, 4 courses, £37.50.
- Ethical Collection: Food.
  See page 10.

On your doorstep
- Castle Howard: elegant temples & lakes, an 18th-century walled garden, seasonal displays of daffodils, magnolias & azaleas
- Sleightholmedale Lodge: hillside garden open for NGS & by appointment

Top tip
Struggling plants often revive if returned to a pot for intensive care

Contact

Anton van der Horst & Phillip Gill
Shallowdale House,
West End,
Ampleforth YO62 4DY

01439 788325
stay@shallowdalehouse.co.uk
www.shallowdalehouse.co.uk

Map: see page 188

Yorkshire

Swinton Park

Grand parkland with a huge walled garden brilliantly redesigned

The house

Swinton is utterly glorious with marble pillars, varnished wood floors, vast arched windows, roaring fires. The drawing room is stupendous, the dining room impressive. Art lines the main corridor, there's a bar in the old chapel and the stables are now home to a cookery school. Bedrooms come in grand country-house style: plush fabrics, huge beds, marble bathrooms, decanters of complimentary gin and whisky. As for the food, game from the estate and vegetables from the garden are plentiful, while hampers can be left in bothies on the estate for walkers wanting a jolly good lunch.

The garden

You have as your playground 200 acres of landscaped parkland surrounded by the Yorkshire Dales. Originally planted by the Danby family in the 1760s, and left to grow wild in the 1970s, the gardens, lakes and parkland are again in pristine order. The four-acre walled garden, once a Christmas tree plantation, is now in full production thanks to Susan Cunliffe-Lister, a highly regarded designer who restored the ornamental walled garden at Burton Agnes. Over 60 varieties of seasonal fruit, vegetables and herbs travel no further than your table, while a huge cutting garden means the house is ever filled with elegant arrangements and heady scents. Take tea or an evening drink on the smooth terrace overlooking the croquet lawn; views reach to Home Lake and the deer park. Further afield there are woodland walks crowded with wildflowers, standing stones, Druids' seats, stone coffins and waterfalls – in perfect keeping with the Romantic tradition – and ancient trees around deep, moody lakes planted in the style of 'Capability' Brown; marked walks are timed for the fit and the not so fit. Birds of prey in the Orangery are exciting for children, while owls, ducks, fish, rabbits and pheasants will delight all.

Details

- Rooms: 25 twins/doubles, 5 suites.
- Price: £175-£290. Suites £300-£370. Half-board from £245.
- Meals: Lunch, 3 courses, £25. Dinner £48. Tasting menu £55.
- Travel Club offer: 25% off room rate Mon-Thurs.

On your doorstep
- Thorp Perrow Arboretum: stunning autumn colours
- Newby Hall Gardens: celebrated borders & sculpture park
- Springtime bluebells & wild garlic along the rivers Ure & Burn

Top tip
Sheep's fleece keeps frost off vulnerable plants & adds nitrogen to the soil

Contact

Mark & Felicity Cunliffe-Lister
Swinton Park,
Swinton,
Ripon HG4 4JH

01765 680900
reservations@swintonpark.com
www.swintonpark.com

Map: see page 188

Millgate House

Long, walled, terraced town garden with exuberant planting

The house

Prepare to be amazed. In every room of the house and in every corner of the garden, the marriage of natural beauty and sophistication exists in a state of bliss. The four Doric columns at the entrance draw you through the hall into the dining room and to views of the Swale Valley. Beds from Heals, period furniture, cast-iron baths, myriad prints and paintings and one double bed so high you wonder how to get onto it. Tim and Austin, both ex-English teachers, both great company, have created something special, and the breakfasts are superb. *Children over ten only.*

The garden

Nothing about the elegant façade of Austin and Tim's home hints at the treasures which lie behind. Wandering into the drawing room you are drawn, magnet-like, to the veranda to discover the full impact of the garden below. A stay at Millgate House without exploring it would be an unforgivable omission; no wonder that when Austin and Tim entered the Royal Horticultural Society's 1995 National Garden Competition they romped away with first prize. This famous walled town garden deserves every last bouquet and adulatory article it has received. A narrow shady lane to one side of the house, adorned with immaculate hostas, introduces the main garden. Here the long terraced grounds, sloping steeply down towards the river and overlooked by the great Norman castle, are divided into a rhythmic series of lush compartments. All is green, with cascades of foliage breaking out into small, sunny open areas before you dive beneath yet more foliage to explore further secret areas. Plantsmanship, a passion for old roses, hostas, clematis, ferns and small trees and a love of many different leaf forms come together triumphantly. As William Blake said: "Exuberance is beauty". If you just want to explore the garden you can phone Austin and Tim to arrange a visit. *NGS, RHS, Good Gardens Guide.*

Details

- Rooms: 2 doubles, 1 twin.
- Price: £110–£145.
- Meals: Restaurant 250 yards.
- Travel Club offer: Free malt whisky in rooms.
- Ethical Collection: Community; Food. See page 10.

On your doorstep
- Newby Hall Gardens: flowering cherries in April/May, magnificent borders in summer, the Autumn Garden for end-of-season pleasures & the national collection of cornus (dogwood)

Top tip
For successful hostas, feed with bonemeal & keep slugs clear

Contact

Austin Lynch & Tim Culkin
Millgate House,
Richmond DL10 4JN

01748 823571
07738 298721 (mobile)
oztim@millgatehouse.demon.co.uk
www.millgatehouse.com

Map: see page 188

Capheaton Hall

A Northumbrian secret – formality, splendour & a working kitchen garden

The house

A glorious approach down a beech-lined drive delivers you to the north front of this important 1668 house with classic Georgian additions. Charming Eliza makes you feel at home among the family portraits and the gleaming furniture. Bedrooms are delightfully quiet and elegant, each one large and light with antiques, soft colours and pristine bathrooms; one with views across the park. Food is locally sourced, vegetables are home-grown and eggs are from their own bantams; eat in if you can. Lots to explore, from craggy rocks to wild fells and plenty of other gardens to visit.

The garden

Eliza, and her husband Will, took over the house and garden in 2008; Capheaton has been in Will's family since the 14th-century. Eliza has taken on the management of the garden with great enthusiasm, although she confesses it was already immaculate when she arrived. The formal grounds consist of nearly four acres of lawns, borders and shrubbery, and a perfect working walled garden with neat vegetable beds and wonderful greenhouses containing peaches, nectarines and figs. A big project is the replanting of the huge border to the west of the garden which Eliza plans to plant in swathes of year-round colour; future plans include planting an avenue of pleached limes leading to the north front of the house. There's much to see and do: an early 19th-century conservatory is a superb example of late Georgian garden design, there are ponds with statues to admire and benches to rest on. Enjoy the view of the front park, the magnificent beeches and oaks of the Hall wood, discover the folly of a chapel, or set off for a quarter of a mile walk down to the lake, alive with ducks. A garden worth revisiting.

Details

- Rooms: 2 doubles. 1 twin.
- Price: £120-£140. Singles £80-£90.
- Meals: Dinner, 4 courses, £30. Supper £20. Pub/restaurant 6 miles.
- Travel Club offer: Tea & homemade cake on arrival 5-6.30pm.

On your doorstep
- Herterton Hall: one acre divided into five parts: topiary, physic garden, flower garden, gazebo & nursery, surrounded by fine stone walls
- Belsay Hall: stunning snowdrops & winter foliage

Top tip
Pollinate peach blossom by dusting with a rabbit tail tied to a bamboo stick

Contact

Eliza & Will Browne-Swinburne
Capheaton Hall,
Capheaton,
Newcastle upon Tyne NE19 2AB

01830 530159
elizab-s@hotmail.co.uk

Map: see page 188

Dumfries & Galloway • Fife • Angus • Argyll & Bute • Highland

Scotland

Scotland

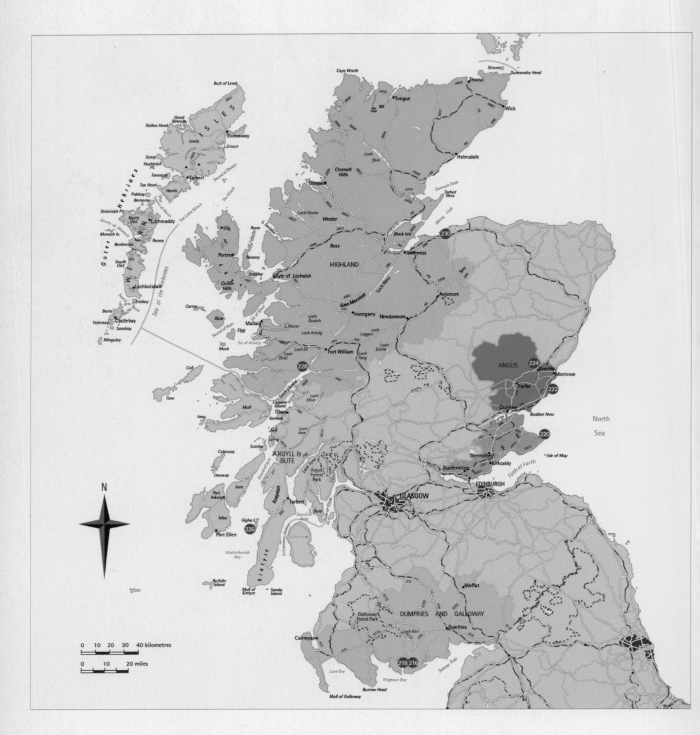

Special places to stay

Glenholme Country House

A great combination of wild garden & structured planting

The house

Jennifer and Laurence thoroughly spoil you in their 1890 house of local stone, a mere stroll from Kirkcudbright with its independent shops. Bedrooms are large and light with antique quilts, vintage fabrics, walk-in showers and happy views. Sink into a comfortable chair in the library with its open fire and thousands of books and CDs, discover old photographs from the Raj, and objects and furniture from all over the world. Eat in if you can: Laurence cooks with flair and the vegetables come from a garden you can take your time exploring; breakfast is when you choose and can include duck eggs.

The garden

In Victorian times these one-and-a-half acres boasted a tennis court, greenhouses, vegetable gardens and swathes of rhododendrons, interspersed with round rose beds and neat shrubs. Jennifer with her artistic eye has softened things hugely; wander at will through the many different areas. By the house, formal stone steps dotted with *Erigeron karvinskianus* lead down to nine long, deep herbaceous borders filled with blowsy cottage garden favourites in pinks, soft purples and whites: aquilegia, astrantia, campanula, hardy geraniums, oriental poppies, alliums for structure and roses for scent. The whole garden is protected by mature beech hedges, the shrubbery is bright with azaleas in spring, and species agapanthus perk up a south-facing wall. The vegetable garden is made up of eight raised beds and is amazingly productive, the orchard produces apples, plums and soft fruit, all for the table with zero food miles. The pond is planted with flag irises, foxgloves, primroses, ranunculus and watercress; rest here with a glass of something and have a think. Later you can walk through the woodland and listen to the resident rooks with their poignant call, or watch the many other birds in and around the garden. Lovely.

Details

- Rooms: 3 doubles, 1 twin.
- Price: £90–£110.
- Meals: Dinner, 3 courses, £28–£30.
- Travel Club offer: 10% off stays of 2 or more nights.

On your doorstep
- Elizabeth MacGregor: just next door, a beautiful walled nursery selling cottage garden plants
- Cally Gardens: talk to knowledgeable plantsman Michael Wickenden

Top tip
Relish your weeds! Add early bittercress & steamed ground elder tips to salads

Contact

Jennifer & Laurence Bristow-Smith
Glenholme Country House, Glenholme,
Tongland Road, Kirkcudbright DG6 4UU

01557 339422
07928 944873 (mobile)
info@glenholmecountryhouse.com
www.glenholmecountryhouse.com

Map: see page 214

The Rookery

Your own secluded patch of Glenholme's lovely garden

The house

You stay in what was the old laundry and servants' quarters; rooms are warm and airy, with a Scandinavian feel in the tongue-and groove wood panelling. The living room has fresh flowers, an open fire, comfy sofa, and lots of books and games; the kitchen is simple but neat as a pin, and if you don't want to cook you can have delicious dinners at the main house. Bedrooms have firm beds and gorgeous fabrics; bathrooms are new and spoiling. Kirkcudbright, with its ancient castle and secluded harbour, is a walkable distance; super beaches are a short drive. *See Glenholme Country House (previous page).*

The garden

Kirkcudbright is known as the St Ives of the north – not only because of the artists who flocked here at the turn of the century, but also for its extremely mild climate. At the Rookery you have your own patch of garden with outdoor furniture and a barbecue surrounded by tall beech hedges: it feels nicely private. Jennifer's aim was to soften this inherited garden; the previous owner was a Scottish rubber planter with a penchant for rigid municipal flower beds and ruthlessly clipped shrubs. Now you wander through a wild wooded area, with Scots pine, chestnuts, beech and bluebells in spring; 40 rooks make their nests here every year. The orchard is much loved and has very productive apple and plum trees; there are also gooseberry, redcurrant, blackcurrant and raspberry bushes whose fruits Jennifer turns into jams and preserves. The best treat, though, is the vegetable garden: raised beds from railway sleepers provide beans galore, peas, curly kale, sweetcorn, celery, asparagus, fresh herbs, rhubarb and beetroot, along with salad leaves of every kind; and you're welcome to help yourselves.

Details

- Rooms: Self-catering cottage for 4.
- Price: £450-£950 per week.
- Meals: Dinner, 3 courses, from £28.
- Travel Club offer: Bottle of wine.

On your doorstep
- Castramont Woods: a fine example of old oak woodland, loved for its bluebells & breeding songbirds
- Corsock House: one-acre garden, with rhododendrons & azaleas in May

Top tip
Recycle old clothing & make a scarecrow to ward off the pigeons

Contact

Jennifer & Laurence Bristow-Smith
The Rookery, Glenholme,
Tongland Road, Kirkcudbright DG6 4UU

01557 339422
07928 944873 (mobile)
info@glenholmecountryhouse.com
www.glenholmecountryhouse.com

Map: see page 214

Cambo House

Inspirational garden with huge romantic borders & dreamy woodland

The house

A Victorian mansion in the grand style, with staff. Magnificent and luxurious are the bedrooms; the yellow room was once used for servicing the dining room, which is more of a banqueting hall – you breakfast here in the summer months. You are welcome to view this, and also the first-floor billiard room and drawing room. There is a delightful sitting room for your use on the ground floor overlooking the fountain. If you B&B in one of the studio apartments for two – Garden (with double) and Orchard (with twin) – both with lovely parkland views, you may come and go as you please.

The garden

A garden of renown, stunningly romantic all year round, and with lots of new initiatives. There is a spectacular carpet of snowdrops in the 70 acres of woodland, now dotted with environmental sculptures; Snowdrops by Starlight is a magical walk enhanced by light and sound. Spring brings an annual Tulip Festival and an exhibition of tulip photography; hundreds of cut blooms fill the tearoom. In summer over a hundred ramblers and climbers, including historic roses, shoot off over bridges and along ropes; walks and talks form part of the annual Rose Festival. A new prairie garden, one of only a handful outside America, is at its best in late summer; the Cambo burn carves its way across the two-acre walled garden where a huge range of herbaceous perennials and roses fill the borders with colour. A willow weeps artfully between a decorative bridge and a Chinese-style summerhouse looks as though it has stepped out of a willow-pattern plate. The potager created in 2001 has matured brilliantly, the hot red and yellow annuals among the vegetables and the herbaceous perennials carrying colour through August. Marvellous.

RHS, SGS, Good Gardens Guide.

Details

- Rooms: 3 doubles, 1 twin, 2 studios for 2 with s/c option.
- Price: £110-£144. Singles £55-£72.
- Meals: Dinner from £45. Pub 2 miles.
- Travel Club offer: 10% off room rate Mon-Thurs.

On your doorstep
- Kellie Castle Gardens: Arts & Crafts walled garden with fruit & veg to buy in autumn
- St Andrews Botanic Gardens: Glory Bush in late summer, fascinating glasshouses open all year

Top tip
Plant crocuses in early autumn, before the mice get hungry

Contact

Sir Peter & Lady Erskine
Cambo House,
Kingsbarns,
St Andrews KY16 8QD

01333 450313
cambo@camboestate.com
www.camboestate.com

Map: see page 214

Ethie Castle

Six developing acres of structure, colour, diversity & wildlife

The house

Kirstin and Adrian are experts at breathing new life into old houses without stripping them of history or character, and their collection of furniture is impressive. Dine in the Tudor kitchen with its walk-in fireplace, admire the 1500 ceiling in the Great Hall, bury yourself in the library, wander the grounds for architectural gems. Bedrooms are comfortable and light, one with a green Art Deco bathroom. Food is a passion for Kirstin: beef from the estate, home-grown vegetables, rare-breed pork from a neighbour. One of Scotland's most beautiful beaches is at the end of the road.

The garden

This garden was started from scratch four years ago, planted for structure, colour and diversity, and with the primary aim of increasing the bird, butterfly and bee population. There are six acres of formal gardens around the house including a walled vegetable garden, a parterre criss-crossed with box hedging, herbaceous borders and a rose garden. Wander across smooth lawns, admire the new fountain and the old folly (1910), visit the glasshouses brimming with ancient vines. Planting is in long-lasting coloured swathes, and especially hardy varieties have been chosen to cope with sea air, wind and cooler temperatures. Twelve hundred mixed hardwood trees have been planted, there is a restored lime avenue, beech hedging and yew walks. The vegetable garden positively bursts: with beans, sweetcorn, chard, three types of potatoes, Jerusalem artichokes, salads, horseradish and soft fruit – raspberries, gooseberries, blackcurrants, redcurrants, melons and grapes – all for the table. There's a lovely summerhouse for an evening drink, and plenty of wildlife to watch: toads, frogs, deer and hares, and birds including tree-creepers and siskins. A garden to visit time and time again. *SGS.*

Details

- Rooms: 2 doubles, 1 twin/double.
- Price: From £95. Singles from £75.
- Meals: Dinner, 4 courses with wine, £30. Packed lunch £10. Pub/restaurant 3 miles.

On your doorstep
- House of Dun: restored to an 1880s Victorian garden; snowdrops in Jan, woodland walks all year
- Pitmuies Gardens: two semi-formal walled gardens shelter a long border, loch walks beckon beneath fine trees

Top tip
Cover vegetables with biodegradable fleece to prevent devastation by bugs & cabbage whites

Contact

Kirstin de Morgan
Ethie Castle,
Inverkeilor,
Arbroath DD11 5SP

01241 830434
kmydemorgan@aol.com
www.ethiecastle.com

Map: see page 214

Newtonmill House

Formal walled gardens with a glorious herbaceous vista

The house

The house and grounds are in perfect order; the owners are warm, charming and discreet. This is a little-known part of Scotland, with glens and gardens to discover; fishing villages, golf courses and deserted beaches, too. Return to a cup of tea in the sitting room or summerhouse, a wander in the lovely walled garden, and a marvellous supper of local produce. Upstairs are crisp sheets, soft blankets, feather pillows, fresh flowers, homemade fruit cake and warm sparkling bathrooms with thick towels. Let this home envelop you in its warm embrace. *Children over ten welcome.*

The garden

Stephen and Rose have been enlarging and enhancing these lovely gardens for 24 years. Borders, beds, lawns, woodland and pastures are bounded by old walls, hedges and burns. At the heart of it all is the walled garden that faces the gracious laird's house, its 'entrance' an iron gate in the shape of a mill wheel, its grass walk bounded by herbaceous borders. Formal box hedges edge rectangular beds where fruit, vegetables and flowers grow in glorious profusion – one full of irises, another of peonies. Another contains a croquet lawn, perfect with a revolving summerhouse and an arbour of honeysuckle and clematis. Espaliered and fan-trained apples, pears and plums clothe the walls, roses clamber and fall in a delicious harmony of scents and hues, a group of Japanese maples shades *Podophyllum hexandrum* and, in a corner, an 18th-century 'doocot' stands, home to happy doves. The heavy soil has been improved over the years with horse and sheep manure; most of the crops are grown with organic principles in mind, and much surplus is given away. Over twenty varieties of potato are grown, the raspberries do famously and, in the woodland areas, primroses, bluebells, narcissi and martagon lilies thrive. *SGS, featured in Scotland for Gardeners.*

Photographs © Roy Summers/Scottish Field

Details

- Rooms: 1 double, 1 twin.
- Price: £96-£115. Singles from £60.
- Meals: Dinner £23-£32. BYO. Packed lunch £10. Pub 3 miles.
- Travel Club offer: 10% off stays of 2 or more nights Nov-May.
- Use your Sawday's Gift Card here.

On your doorstep
- Glamis Castle: bulbs grace the avenue in spring; summer/autumn are a riot of colour; chase the Winter Trail & warm up with hot chocolate
- Pitmuies Gardens: old-fashioned roses, massed delphiniums & an alpine meadow

Top tip
Plant tight borders for rich tapestries of colour

Contact

Rose & Stephen Rickman
Newtonmill House,
Brechin DD9 7PZ

01356 622533
07793 169482 (mobile)
rrickman@srickman.co.uk
www.newtonmillhouse.co.uk

Map: see page 214

Argyll & Bute

Achamore House

Fifty acres on a Hebridean island devoted to rare-species rhododendrons

The house

No traffic jams here, tucked between the mainland and Islay. Despite its grandeur – turrets, Arts & Crafts doors, plasterwork ceilings – Achamore is not stuffy and neither are Don and Emma. A coastal skipper, he can take you to sea, or over to other islands in his Redbay RIB. Find warm wood panelling and light-washed rooms, huge bedrooms with shuttered windows, oversize beds, heavy antiques, iPods, music. You get the run of the house – billiard room, library, large lounge, TV room (great for kids). With vast gardens and a quiet beach it's ideal for big parties or gatherings.

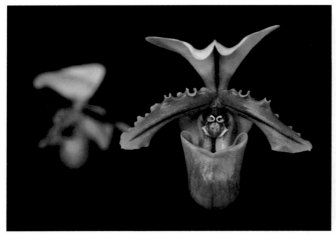

The garden

Don is probably the luckiest gardener in the world: the Isle of Gigha Trust own and have responsibility for these 52 acres, Don just gets to live in the middle of it all and, in his greenhouse, grow the tropical orchids that are his love – some of the orchids are used to make flower essences which Don sells. Visitors to the house can wander at will through mature woodland, stroll the walled garden, visit the pond garden and, in July and August, have home-baked cakes and tea in the tea tent: there's a huge variety of specimen plants, shrubs, some rare trees and roses. Established in 1944 by Sir James Horlick, then owner of the island, the garden is most famous for rhododendrons, camellias and azaleas – the 'Horlick Collection' has gained international recognition among horticulturists, but it was becoming neglected. Now the Trust have raised a sum of money for restoration work to start: over the next three years they will be replacing the drainage systems, rebuilding the shelter belt, replacing paths and greenhouses and restocking the gardens; locals call this place the 'jewel in the crown' of Gigha and it's easy to see why. Lovely views, abundant wildlife, a stunning plant collection. Well worth a visit.

Details

- Rooms: 4 doubles, 2 twins/doubles, 2 singles, 1 family room.
- Price: £90–£130. Singles from £35.
- Meals: Pub/restaurant 1 mile.
- Travel Club offer: Free pick-up from ferry port.

On your doorstep
- In a greenhouse on the lawns: over 600 orchids, including the cloud-forest orchids of South America, & the amazing bulbophyllums found throughout the tropics

Top tip
Phragmipediums, fabulous slipper orchids from South America, are easy-growers in any temperature you are comfortable with

Contact

Don Dennis & Emma Rennie
Achamore House,
Isle of Gigha PA41 7AD

01583 505400
gigha@atlas.co.uk
www.achamorehouse.com

Map: see page 214

Ard Daraich

Huge ericaceous garden in a spectacular setting

The house

You cross Loch Linnhe on the Corran ferry to reach Ard Daraich (Gaelic for 'the house beneath the oak'). Constance Spry used to holiday at this stone Highland home – now Norrie and Anna fill the place with intelligent chat, creativity and laughter. Bursting bookshelves lead to comfortable, antiquey bedrooms, one downstairs, one under the eaves with a delicious view from the adjacent roll top bath. Drink in the views from Ben Nevis to Mull, sit still on the beach or tramp the old drove road that passes your door. Peaceful.

The garden

Constance Spry's influence is found to this day: rich herbaceous borders circle the house along with two rills ('the Blue and White Nile'!), built to drain water away. Norrie's parents gardened here for 40 years; now he and Anna, creative types, passionate about plants and people, continue to nurture the eight-acre Hill Garden. It is home to a startling collection of over 1,000 rhododendron species and hybrids, hundreds of acers (the Maclarens are members of the Maple Society) and sorbus, many donated by Lord Ridley, owner of the national collection. Seeds and plants are sent from all over the world, making this one of the best ericaceous collections in Scotland.

The tough Highland terrain (gravel, granite, peat) benefits from imaginative gardening, and by allowing indigenous birch trees to flourish, the pair have cultivated a microclimate in which interesting and rare plants – often brought on from South Korean seeds – thrive. A maze of paths meander about; opposite the house *Liquidambar styraciflua*, *Stachyurus* and the handkerchief tree dance in the wind. Bracing walks shoot off in all directions and there are breathtaking views. Eggs from rare-breed hens and home-grown soft fruits appear at your breakfast table. The silence is interrupted only by birdsong.

Details

- Rooms: 3 doubles.
  Self-catered studio for 2.
- Price: From £75. Singles £60.
  Studio from £400 p.w.
- Meals: Restaurants nearby.

On your doorstep
- Loch Linnhe: stunning sea loch – breathtaking sunsets during the summer months & year-round wilderness
- Glen Coe: walking & climbing heaven, surrounded by wild & precipitous mountains

Top tip
Plant tulip bulbs in staggered layers for compact colour

Contact

Norrie & Anna Maclaren
Ard Daraich,
Ardgour,
Fort William PH33 7AB

01855 841384
annaraven@btinternet.com
www.arddaraich.co.uk

Map: see page 214

Boath House

Twenty-two acres of parkland, woodland, streams, lake & walled garden

The house

It's luxury all the way at the Boath House: a Michelin star in the dining room, a library that doubles as a whisky bar, a roaring fire in the drawing room, and walls crammed with exceptional art. Country-house bedrooms are no less alluring. One comes with a couple of claw-foot baths, all have rich fabrics, warm colours, white robes and bowls of fruit; two on the lower ground in the old kitchens have vaulted ceilings... and there's a treatment room for pampering. Inverness, Cromarty, Aviemore and Culloden are all close and there's golf at Nairn and Dornoch.

The garden

Energetic and clever, Wendy tucked a diploma in residential landscape architecture under her belt and got seriously stuck into these 22 acres as soon as she'd waved her wand over the house. Woodland and parkland, lawns, lake and streams and a two-acre walled garden are now glorious and you are free to wander at will. The Victorian walled garden is where the main bulk of the work is concentrated, to provide fresh produce for the restaurant: an orchard with varieties of apples, plums, cherries, pears and nuts, parterres for soft fruit, herbs and fresh vegetables, bantam eggs and honey from their own hives... zero food miles. In winter the greenhouse is heated to enable successional planting to continue. New borders showcase Wendy's passion for special grasses inspired by the best contemporary garden designers, mature trees include copper beech, oak, lime, acer and Scots pine. A wildflower meadow (home to copious butterflies, dragonflies, damselflies and the occasional deer) constantly changes colour during the growing season. The serene two-acre lake is fed from a stream and has been extended to include a bog garden with islands and a bridge; you may spot a brown trout or other indigenous fish. Lovely.

Details

- Rooms: 4 doubles, 4 twins/doubles.
- Price: £190-£260.
- Meals: Lunch from £24.
  Dinner, 6 courses, £70.
  Packed lunch by arrangement.
- Travel Club offer: A personal tour of the gardens by either Wendy Matheson or the head gardener. Must be pre-arranged.

On your doorstep
- Culbin Forest: get a treetop view from the wooden tower on the forest's highest hill
- Brodie Castle Gardens: unique & famous collection of daffodils in spring & year-round hides for wildlife-watching

Top tip
Never be frightened to experiment with colour – happy accidents rule!

Contact

Don & Wendy Matheson
Boath House,
Auldearn, Nairn IV12 5TE

01667 454896
info@boath-house.com
www.boath-house.com

Map: see page 214

Spend memorable days visiting Scotland's most remarkable and beautiful gardens which open to the public for Scotland's Gardens Scheme and support a variety of truly worthy charities.

For more information refer to our website:
www.gardensofscotland.org

 Scotland's Gardens Scheme

Gardens open for charity

© Ray Cox

Charity No. SC011337

Alastair Sawday's other guides

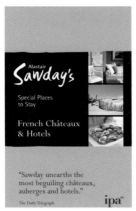

Alastair Sawday Publishing has created over twenty-four *Special Places to Stay* **and** *Go Slow* **guides. Each one of our 5,000 properties has been visited, and chosen, by us because we like it, and its owners.**

Why are we different? We take huge pleasure from finding people and places that do their own thing – brilliantly; places that are unusual and follow no trends, places of peace and beauty, and people who are kind and interesting – and genuine.

Our books are founded upon a passion for the unpretentious, the authentic and the unique. Our criteria for deciding whether a place is special may appear obscure – we have no star system and do not include somewhere just because it has all the right 'facilities'. The things that count, for us, are people, architecture, history, views and, above all, atmosphere. A faded 17th-century palace run by a generous, spirited family would be chosen in preference over a slick, designer hotel with all the five-star trimmings but super-cool staff.

We like owners who know what they're doing but, perhaps more importantly, we like owners who enjoy what they're doing and who are generous with little things as well as big ones. We like flexibility and a willingness to consider people's needs. We know that an encounter with genuine kindness and an easy welcome live longer in the memory than any number of 'facilities' that have earned gold or silver awards.

We are delighted, too, that so many of our owners care deeply about good food. Much of what they serve – be it in a B&B, a hotel or an inn – is local, seasonal or organic.

So we have many more jewels in our crown, quite apart from the hundred-odd special places in this book.

Use our website to find out lots more about the places in this book, including directions to each property.

www.sawdays.co.uk

Book sales: 01275 395431

Garden blogs & garden classics

Gardeners like to share things from their gardens, including their thoughts. For the writer, a blog is the perfect way to record and share. For the reader, it's a way to find information and inspiration. The only problem is, one blog leads to another, for every blogger has his/her rollcall of favourites. Before you know it, darkness has descended and you've forgotten to mulch the perennials. The best bloggers create their own little intimate worlds.

My Tiny Plot: mytinyplot.co.uk

The diary of a small vegetable patch in Bath. Gardening philosophy includes considering slugs and snails your friends (as far as humanely possible), growing flowers to encourage the bees and doing organic until it becomes a pain. Ten jobs for every month, encouragement aplenty and recipes, too.

LaetitiaMaklouf: laetitiamaklouf.com

A lifestyle blog (with small bookshop attached) from the author of *The Virgin Gardener*, with tips firmly aimed at the stylish gardener. October: "Plant some wallflowers – lovely groundcover all winter and knock-out scent in the spring. I've bought some plants from a nursery (it really is okay to do this...you're not cheating). Bung them in the ground (or in a pot, why not?) and enjoy. Lastly, one word... Hippeastrum. I know these bulbs are expensive, but it's so worth investing in a few and putting them in pots, say three per month until January for total indoor drama between winter and spring."

Midnight Brambling: lialeendertz.wordpress.com

A blogger for *The Guardian*, with an 80' garden and an allotment not just for growing food on but "to mark the seasons, celebrating summer with barbecues and winter with wassailing, and showing the kids what the turning of the year really means." Lia always has one eye on the environment. Note her dandelion root fertiliser recipe for lawns - a sustainable alternative to rock phosphate, "a finite source which we are charging through at a rate of knots."

An Artist's Garden: artistsgarden.co.uk

"I really must stop shopping on the internet in the middle of the night when I cannot sleep as I was totally seduced by Eremurus 'Cleopatra' and before you could say 'foxtail lily' some had found their way into my virtual shopping basket." A textile artist's garden from the west coast of Wales: interesting, engaging and full of great photos.

The Inelegant Gardener: inelegantgardener.blogspot.com

"It's around this time of year that the tips of the branches of trees and hedges take on a golden highlight. They always remind me very much of highlights in George Michael's Wham era hair. I don't know why. I was never much of a Wham fan." Quirky observations and pictures are accompanied by quirky captions: "Actaea simplex. Cimicifuga, its former name, was a name that you could roll around your mouth; Actaea sounds much spikier."

Blogging from Blackpitts Garden: blackpitts.co.uk

An irreverent "depository for the random thoughts" of James Alexander-Sinclair, garden designer. "As I mentioned last week I have had bulbs landing on doorsteps all over the shop and have had to rush about scattering. In the past two days, for example, I have either self-scattered or organised the scattering of somewhere in the region of 11,000 bulbs in six different places ranging from the far Cotswolds to the nether reaches of lower Leicestershire. I was hoping to plant roses as well but the rose supplier has disappeared without trace (see past crossnesses and grumpling in previous posts) and has not answered telephone calls or emails for over a month."

Miss Pickering: misspickering.blogspot.com

Not strictly a gardener, more a "florist, cook and gin drinker". "An appeal to all florists and brides, please can we calm down on the 'Amnesia' usage? It is such a beautiful rose, that when I first encountered it a few years, I thought I would never be able to love anything else again. Now my love for them is fast dwindling, they are everywhere, in every bridal magazine, every 'stylist' is using them, and I fear they are losing their cache." Footnote: 'Amnesia' is not a good garden rose – but the grey-lilac 'Intermezzo' makes a fair substitute.

Gardenersclick.com

A Facebook for gardening and allotment enthusiasts. Dip in and out of the chat, share your ups and downs, read the blogs, peruse the profiles ("I am pre WW2 and first set foot on my father's allotment in 1944 when I was knee-high to a grasshopper"). You'll never be alone again.

In Your Garden Vita Sackville West

Illuminating month by month extracts from Vita's contributions to *The Observer* from 1947 to 1961. Rich in gardening tips from the legendary Sissinghurst. Also in tape form.

The Essential Earthman: Henry Mitchell on Gardening

Opening lines: "As I write this, it's about time for another summer storm to smash the garden to pieces, though it may hold off until the phlox, tomatoes, daylilies, and zinnias are in full sway." Refreshing take on the ups and downs of gardening from essayist and columnist on *The Washington Post* in the 1970s.

Dear Friend and Gardener
Beth Chatto & Christopher Lloyd

An engaging exchange of letters between Beth Chatto, who wrested her garden from wilderness in East Anglia, and the late Christopher Lloyd, whose Great Dixter remains a place of pilgrimage. It's all here, from battles with hailstorms in June to matted Biddy-Biddy, "so tiresome in your socks" in February.

Green Thoughts: A Writer in the Garden
Eleanor Perenyi

The writer is as enchanting and informative about worms in her Connecticut garden as she is about the horticultural exploration of the Spanish Conquisadors.

Gardening for all

"The love of gardening is a seed once sown that never dies."
Gertrude Jekyll 1843-1932

Gertrude was lucky enough to enjoy robust health for most of her long gardening life. But what if something prevents you from working in your garden? Accidents, illness or just plain old age can put a halt to a gardener's pleasure, leaving one marooned indoors and prone to depression.

But there is light for gardeners who are no longer able to manage on their own, thanks to some inspiring organisations that recognise how wide the benefits of gardening are. It is not just the obvious physical exercise/fresh air combination that works magic; evidence shows that mental health can be improved, self-esteem raised and sadness lifted. The following charities are determined to keep people gardening, whatever their personal circumstances.

Gardening for the Disabled, a voluntary organisation, was formed over forty years ago in order "that people may continue to garden in spite of advancing illness, age or disability". Funds are raised through donations, legacies and fund-raising events. Those helped by the trust include:

- gardeners with chronic back or hip trouble
- a wide range of visual, physical and mental disabilities
- people who need to reorganise gardens because of failing health
- residents in long-stay hospitals or homes who share a garden

The trust can offer help by adapting private gardens to meet the special needs of the disabled; making grants towards tools, raised beds and greenhouses; providing help with special gardens in hospitals and schools; distributing information on garden aids and techniques and providing a magazine forum for disabled gardeners. www.gardeningfordisabledtrust.org.uk

In October 2009 the Southern Spinal Injuries Trust launched an appeal to raise funds to build a garden at The Duke of Cornwall Spinal Treatment Centre in Salisbury. Most patients who suffer a spinal injury are in hospital for between nine months and a year, so having an outdoor space as a refuge and as a leisure and social space is vital.

Tracy Wilson, the BBC Radio Cornwall gardening correspondent, is designing the Jubilee Garden to be accessible for beds and wheelchairs, and within sight of the nursing staff.

Annie Maw (pictured here in her own garden) has been confined to a wheelchair since a riding accident

and spent several months at the unit. Longing for fresh air, she asked to be taken outside, but the only place to wheel her bed was the car park. Annie, now a tireless campaigner for the fund, was undaunted. "I had a brief chance to see the blue sky and feel the sun on my cheeks, and I know how much a proper garden will improve the lives of those trying to come to terms with a catastrophe."

It is also hoped that patients will learn the pleasure of growing their own vegetables, which can then be harvested and cooked in the specially modified kitchen in the unit.

To learn more about the Jubilee Garden, or to donate to the appeal, visit www.ssit.org.uk

Thrive is a small national charity that believes passionately in the power of gardening to change lives. It first launched its Carry On Gardening website in

2003, using thirty years of experience in helping disabled people to start or continue gardening.

As well as giving advice on how to garden to people with physical problems and offering practical tips on special tools, Thrive runs its own gardening projects (one pictured below) and maintains contact list for schemes in the UK so you can search for those local to you. Two projects have been launched to help older people with little or no family support in rural communities, who would otherwise be isolated.

Thrive also believes that gardening has the power to improve emotional as well as physical health. Its booklet *'Harnessing the mood-boosting power of gardening'* provides information for those "interested in the benefits of gardening for emotional wellbeing".

The testimonies on the website speak for themselves. www.carryongardening.org.uk

A plant well-planted is a plant half-grown

Struggling plants often revive if returned to a pot for intensive care

When planting broad beans, line trench with trimmed horse mane to deter moles and mice

For hardy, long-lived hedges, choose yew

Plant garlic around roses to deter pests

Prune fruit-bearing stems of redcurrant efficiently & then gather the fruit

Plant crocuses in early autumn, before the mice get hungry

Our gardeners' top tips...

Plant garlic under peach trees to prevent leaf curl

For instant screening, plant a row of pre-grown pleached limes

Cayenne pepper paste around young tulip bulbs deters hungry voles

Pollinate peach blossom by dusting with a rabbit tail tied to a bamboo stick

Plant borage near veg to encourage bees

A thick mulch is a back's best friend

Feed the birds in winter and they will stay for summer and eat your pests

Copper tape under the rim of a hosta pot & pebbles on the soil guarantee no slugs

To deter deer, hang soap over their favourite plants

To preserve roses, hold cut stems over a candle for ten seconds and put into deep, cold water

Avoid slug pellets - keep Indian Runner ducks instead

Leave seed heads on perennials for the birds during winter

Alliums like Globemaster give early-season interest

If you're short of time grow rambling roses rather than hybrids

Make a slug barrier around veg with used coffee grounds - not too close!

Be vigilant: keep your garden neat with nowhere for slugs & bugs to hide

Water sparingly to help plants cope better with a dry spell

Conkers make excellent mothballs; spiders hate them too

Town index